THE WORD PROCESSING HANDBOOK

A Step-by-Step Guide to Automating Your Office

by
Katherine Aschner

Illustrations by Kerry Leimer/Creative Services

Cartoons by Fred Birchman

KNOWLEDGE INDUSTRY PUBLICATIONS, INC.
WHITE PLAINS, NEW YORK

VAN NOSTRAND REINHOLD COMPANY
NEW YORK CINCINNATI TORONTO LONDON MELBOURNE

The Word Processing Handbook:
A Step-by-Step Guide to Automating Your Office

Library of Congress Cataloging in Publication Data

Aschner, Katherine.
   The word processing handbook.

   (Office productivity series)
   Bibliography: p.
   Includes index.
   1. Word processing (Office practice)—Handbooks, manuals, etc.   I. Leimer, Kerry.   II. Birchman, Fred.
III. Title.   IV. Series.
HF5548.115.A8   1982b   652   82-18729
ISBN 0-86729-039-0 (soft)

All rights reserved. No part of this work covered by the copyright hereon may be reproduced or used in any form or by any means—graphic, electronic, or mechanical, including photocopying, recording, taping, or information storage and retrieval systems—without written permission of the publisher.

Printed in the United States of America

Copyright © 1980 by Self-Counsel Press Inc. (U.S.A.)

This edition published 1983 by Knowledge Industry Publications, Inc., 701 Westchester Ave., White Plains, NY 10604, and distributed to the trade by Van Nostrand Reinhold Company Inc., 135 West 50th St., New York, NY 10020.

Cloth and spiral editions published 1982 by Knowledge Industry Publication, Inc., by arrangement with International Self-Counsel Press Ltd., 306 W. 25th St., North Vancouver, B.C., Canada V7N 2G1.

16 15 14 13 12 11 10 9 8 7 6 5 4 3 2 1

Table of Contents

List of Tables and Figures ii
Foreword 1
   1. Word Processing and Data Processing 3
   2. The Types of Equipment Available 9
   3. Case Studies 19
   4. When to Use WP 30
   5. Defining Your Workload 36
   6. Interpreting the Results of the Study 47
   7. Setting Up Shop 63
   8. The Art of Acquiring Word Processors 86
   9. Equipment Evaluation Criteria 93
  10. Data Processing with a Word Processor 126
  11. Optical Character Readers 147
  12. Photocomposition 155
  13. Electronic Mail 166
Glossary 178
Publications for Further Information 188
Index 190
About the Author 192

List of Tables and Figures

Figure 2.1	Electronic Typewriter	10
Figure 2.2	Non-VDT Word Processor	13
Figure 2.3	VDT Word Processor	15
Figure 2.4	Diagram of a Shared-Resource System	17
Figure 2.5	Shared-Resource Workstation	18
Table 6.1	Daily Production Values	52
Table 6.2	Weighting Factors	52
Table 6.3	Secretarial Workload Distibution	57
Figure 7.1	Endless Loop Dictation System	72
Figure 7.2	Distributable Media Dictation Equipment	74
Table 7.1	Line/Page Relationships	85
Figure 9.1	Diagram of Diskette and Disk Pack	105
Figure 10.1	Flow Chart of System	142-145
Figure 11.1	OCR Reader	150
Figure 12.1	Examples of Typefonts	156
Figure 12.2	WP/Photocomposition Interface Chart	160
Figure 12.3	WP/Photocomposer "Black Box" Interface	161
Figure 12.4	Photocomposer/Typesetter	162
Figure 13.1	Facsimile Transceiver	172

Foreword

You probably bought this book for one of two reasons. The first is that you just want to know what office automation is all about. You are interested in word processing and how it fits with data processing. You need to decide if this technology is right for you.

The second reason would be that you have already decided that you need word processing technology. Now you need help selecting the right machines for your business.

Either way, you have come to the right place.

This book is written as a "how to" guide. The focus is not on small business or large business, but on problems and solutions. Anyone who wants to use word processing — called WP for short — can use this book. It follows a step-by-step approach. It contains the tools you need to become your own consultant.

Chapters 1 through 3 explain what word processing is and how it can be used. Chapters 4 through 6 tell how to determine what kind of machines you need and how many. Chapter 7 describes how to set up operations. Chapters 8 and 9 deal with evaluating and selecting machines.

Offices do not live by word processing alone. They often require supplements of data processing (DP), electronic communications and typesetters in their diets. These additional items can be very important in getting the most from your word processing system. The final four chapters of this book discuss these technologies as supplements to word processing systems. The emphasis is on how they work, when to use them and what to look for. Beyond that, each of these technologies is a subject unto itself, worthy of its own book. For those who want to broaden their knowledge of office systems, a suggested reading list is included at the end of the book.

A word about jargon: word processing thrives on it. And I agree that although technology may streamline the office, it does nothing for the language. Nevertheless, I use these terms of the trade throughout.

In dealing with vendors, it is useful to be able to speak the technical language. It also gives you credibility in your own organization. The glossary at the back of the book defines all of these terms.

My approach to technology is this: use everything you need but not everything you can. This book will help you to tell the difference.

1
Word Processing and Data Processing

The best way to understand word processing and its connection with small computers is to take a look at its history. The story goes from typewriters to power typewriters and continues all the way to microprocessors.

TYPEWRITERS

WP is part of a continuum that started with typewriters. Businesses switched from longhand to typewriters because typewriters produced better looking text and were faster. Automation has increased those advantages dramatically. But the underlying rationale remains the same.

POWER TYPEWRITERS

The first step in evolution from typewriter to word processing came with the introduction of paper-tape powered typewriters. These machines used a standard typewriter keyboard to punch a paper tape. A typical example was the Dura Mach 10. A typist could key in a form letter once and replay the tape over and over again, inserting variable information such as names and addresses. The machine was programmed to stop at all the right places.

Power typewriters produced nicer looking letters than preprinted forms. They were also a lot faster than typists manually retyping all those letters. However, there were some serious limitations. The paper tape was fine until a mistake was made. Then you had to splice tapes to remove the error or make some other complex adjustment.

There were other drawbacks, too. The variable information, like names and addresses, always had to be in the same place and roughly the same length. The tape couldn't add or delete whole words or sentences. Finally, there was the problem of the torn tape. Once that long snake of paper was ripped, you were back to splicing, or worse.

HARD-WIRED TEXT EDITORS

True word processing arrived in 1964, when IBM introduced the Magnetic Tape Selectric Typewriter (MTST). It was what we would now call a hard-wired machine. All the functions of the system were imprinted permanently on internal circuit boards.

Unlike power typewriters, the MTST used magnetic rather than paper tape to store keystrokes. Now, you could erase or add whole sentences. You could even insert information in the middle of a letter. This was done by logging the exact place on the magnetic (mag) tape where the insert was to occur. The new information, usually recorded at the end of the original letter, was also carefully logged. By switching back and forth from one spot on the tape to the other, a finished letter could be produced that contained both new and old text in perfect order.

The addition of magnetic media meant that typists could now edit and revise their documents. This was the first real difference between power typewriters and word processors.

There were also other advantages. The mag tapes were much more compact than the paper tapes. Longer documents could be recorded and stored. The tapes were housed in cartridges. No more worries about accidental tears. The tapes could be reused.

Nevertheless, the MTST and other hard-wired systems that followed were far from perfect. Because they relied on circuit boards, they had very limited machine intelligence. In computer terms, this meant that they could perform only limited tasks: principally, playing back stored information. If you wanted proportional spacing (which allocates more space to an m than an i), these older machines couldn't handle it.

Tape, because it stored everything sequentially, was slow. And all that logging made it even slower. In many ways, the MTST was still a close cousin of the power typewriter.

MICROPROCESSOR SYSTEMS

In the remaining years of the sixties, any number of improvements to the MTST concept were made. Magnetic cards were introduced. These eliminated most logging by storing each page of text on its own card; page 42 was much easier to find. The editing features were improved, making it easier to revise long documents. However, the introduction of microprocessors — or very small computers — into the works of the word processor made the final break with the power typewriters of old.

Microprocessor-controlled systems offer three principal advantages over the old hard-wired machines. One, they greatly expand the machine's capacity for work. The machines can be programmed to handle more tasks, and these tasks can be far more complex. For example, you can ask a WP system to change a misspelled name throughout a contract. The word processor will automatically find all the incorrect entries, make the changes and adjust the spacing of the lines as needed.

Second, computers give the systems enough power to handle video displays. The displays, in turn, make the machines easier to use. More about that later.

The third advantage of using microprocessors is that the machines are programmable. In the old days, when you pushed the print button, the print circuit was activated and the machine printed. The only way to add new capabilities was physically to add new circuit boards — not a very practical thing to do. In a programmable machine, the manufacturer writes a program — a set of machine instructions — that tells the machine what to do. When you hit the print button, the print program is set in motion. To add new capabilities, the manufacturer adds new programs. Frequently, these are recorded on the word processor's magnetic storage media and can be sent by mail. The limits to what the word processor can do are in the program capacity of the microprocessor and the imagination of the manufacturer — and neither seems to be stretched at the moment.

Initially, the WP manufacturer provided all the programs, which are often referred to as software. This is still true for the text-editing software. However, once a computer is built into the system, it is a logical step to make some of its capacity available to you, the user. You can use this capacity to run your own programs for anything a computer can do: billing, inventory, receivables, or whatever. At this point, the evolution of word processing has come full circle: both word processing and data processing are available in a single system.

THE DIFFERENCE BETWEEN WP AND DP

This is a good time to examine where WP stops and DP begins. In terms of equipment, the answer is difficult. Many systems offer both. But there is a functional difference, and this is important to understand.

Word processing refers to text: letters, reports and any narrative material. Charts and forms also fall in this category, although the information they carry may involve data processing. Basic WP operations include formatting text, reusing standard text or formats in repetitive documents and editing long documents. During editing, the text may be rearranged substantially. The end product is a document which is meant to be read in its entirety, and in the order presented.

Data processing, for our purposes, concerns itself with information. Either the information itself is rearranged in some way, or there is a computational problem to solve. For example, a store's inventory may be kept on a computer. Periodically, the inventory is updated to reflect sales and new items. Sometimes the entire list is printed out by department, sometimes by supplier name, and sometimes by how long the items have been on the shelf. Sometimes only selected items are printed out, in order to compare sales activity for two similar products. That all comes under the heading of rearrangement. When gross sales, net sales, taxes and commissions are figured, that's computation.

Of course, there is much more to data processing than that. For science, engineering and manufacturing, our definition falls short. But this book is concerned with offices and office uses. For the kinds of systems discussed here, this is the definition we will use.

THE USERS' ADVANTAGE

What does all this mean for you? Word processing still is improving on what typewriters have always done best: that is, produce high-quality text quickly. Today, however, word processors add new dimensions of quality to the finished product. These include justified margins and proportional spacing, special formatting and other ways to make the output look attractive and professional. For marketing, sales and personnel applications, the advantages are obvious.

In terms of speed, the machines simplify editing, cut the routine out of most typing jobs, and print three or more times faster than the old MTSTs. With the addition of data processing, a single system can handle all your communications and information requirements — the limit to its use is truly your own creativity and self-discipline.

Who can take advantage of this technology? Anyone, including you. In the old days, the size of the budget determined whether you could use automation. Today, it is the size of the problem rather than the size of the budget that counts.

There are systems on the market in the range of every user from the small business to the large corporation.

COSTS

Several factors make this expanding marketplace possible. The cost of technology is being driven down by the revolution in microelectronics. Without becoming technical, there are two factors that contribute to this: miniaturization and cheaper production methods. Their impact can be seen by looking at the following chart of minicomputer costs, based on information developed by Digital Equipment Corporation:

Year	Space occupied	Cost
1950	2500 sq. ft.	Incalculable
1960	80 sq. ft.	$120,000
1968	4 sq. ft.	$10,000
1975	18 sq. in.	$650
1982	8 sq. in.	$300

Logic costs, the cost of the actual computer itself, are dropping about 25% a year. Memory costs, the cost of storing information, are dropping about 40% a year. The cost of systems, the finished product, is dropping about 10% to 17% a year. The reason systems costs are not dropping as fast is basically people. The expense of designing, programming, marketing and servicing goes up even though the hardware costs go down.

PRODUCTIVITY

This brings us to the next point: people. Taking the entire work force into account, personnel costs are increasing about 5% a year. For white-collar office workers, the increase is generally greater. This wouldn't be such a problem if office workers' productivity rose at the same rate. So far, it has not. In the past 20 years, according to government statistics, farm and factory workers' productivity has doubled; white collar productivity has risen only 5%. The difference is largely attributable to the use of automation. The office will have to include automation, both for principals (professionals, administrators, authors) and for support staff. We can no longer afford to do otherwise.

One final point, and then our mini-history of WP and related computers will be complete. It's true that all of these systems are getting smaller and cheaper. But there's more to it than that. They are also much easier to use. As the logic capacity — the computer power — of systems increases, more and more sophistication is built in. Where you used to have to remember a whole sequence of steps to reverse two paragraphs, now you just push a button.

Similarly, you can ask complex questions of computers without first writing a special one-time-only program. The machines are now so smart that you don't have to be a programmer to use one. You just have to be smart enough to put it to work.

That's what this book is all about. It will help you decide whether you need any equipment at all. It will explain the differences between word and data processing, and help you decide which one (or both) is right for you. The most common mistake most users make is buying the wrong machine for the job. This book will keep you out of that trap.

2

The Types of Equipment Available

Now that we have an overview of word processing — where it fits in the office scheme — it's time to get down to specifics. This chapter discusses the types of equipment available. The next chapter provides case examples of how they are used.

There are four categories of word processing equipment. These are differentiated by increasing storage capacity (for more and longer documents) and increasing capabilities (for formatting, adding to, and even reorganizing text, as well as for data processing).

It is useful to understand the basic differences between the various levels. They illustrate the types of work for which WP equipment is suited. The price generally increases from level to level, although as new machines enter the market they often break established price barriers. There are also overlaps, meaning that some machines are hard to fit in a niche.

ELECTRONIC TYPEWRITERS

The most basic word processing machine is the electronic typewriter. It looks very much like a standard electric typewriter with some extra keys for word processing functions. (See Figure 2.1.)

Electronic typewriters allow typists to do formatting that they cannot accomplish with their standard machines. For example, the electronic typewriters offer right- and left-margin justification (the ability to produce straight margins on both sides of the page). Coupled with proportional spacing, the finished product is an exceptionally professional looking document.

Electronic typewriters also are labor savers. Depending on the make and model, they can center page headings or line up columns of numbers automatically. This last feature, called automatic decimal alignment, is particularly efficient.

Figure 2.1 Electronic Typewriter

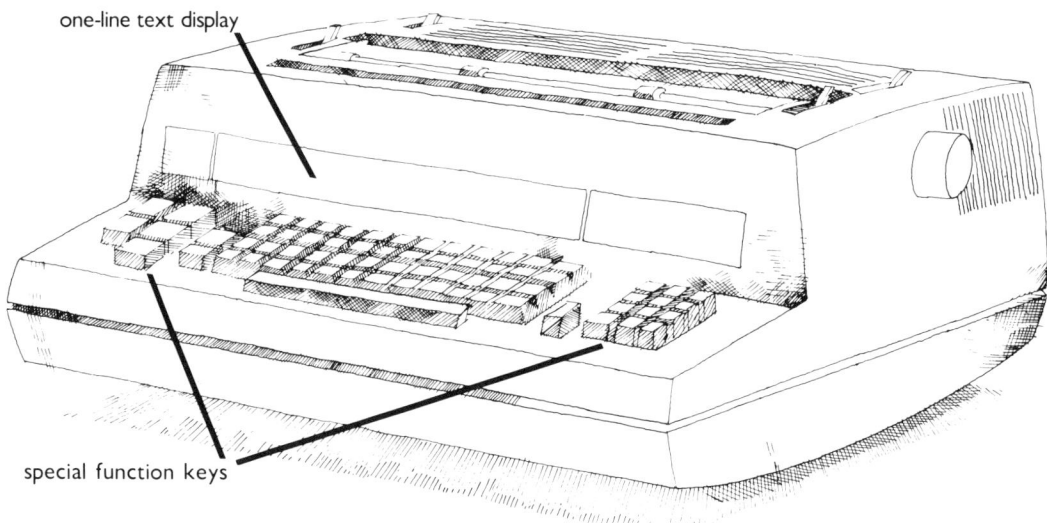

The typist establishes tab stops for each column of numbers. To make an entry, the typist hits the tab key and types the number. The electronics of the machine stores the number until it is fully typed (signalled by hitting the tab key again), and then automatically lines up the units, tens, etc., in the correct place. The time savings results from not having to plan the starting column for each number.

These features illustrate one of the principal attributes of word processing: the ability to enhance the appearance (the quality) of a given document without placing a burden on the typist. Even without the storage and reuse of information, which is the more traditional application, WP can make a valuable contribution. Although some people do not consider machines without storage as true word processors, in actual fact they are.

Since electronic typewriters were first introduced, of course, they have undergone some remarkable developments. Several models have enough internal memory to store a signature block, a standard closing paragraph, or even all of the tab and line spacings for a frequently used form. (This last feature frees the typist from having to set up the tabs each time the form is used.) More sophisticated models will store anywhere from 7 to 15 pages, and some offer telecommunications as well.

Additionally, some electronic typewriters may offer a single line display. This is very useful during editing. For example, to correct a misspelled word, the typist must first find the line and then the character within the word. Without the display, the typist must print the line to know what text the machine is looking at in its memory. Once the change is made, the line must be reprinted to verify that it was done correctly. With the display, the entire printing process can be bypassed, because the display shows the typist what is happening in memory. If "stup" is changed to "stop," the typist can see it happen.

For purposes of this book, electronic typewriters will be defined as any typewriter offering automatic formatting (beyond what a correcting selectric or similar typewriter can do). This includes all machines with limited, non-removable storage. In other words, whether a machine offers a few lines or 100 pages of storage, if the capacity is fixed and the memory cannot be separated from the machine, it is considered an electronic typewriter. Not all equipment vendors will agree with this definition, but the significance of an absolute storage limit is so great that it merits defining a class of equipment.

Electronic typewriters offer one principal advantage: low cost. Some are only marginally more expensive than standard electric typewriters. Correctly matched to the right kind of work — usually in an executive setting, or perhaps in a marketing organization — they may accomplish a great deal with a minimum investment. Several typists can be equipped with electronic typewriters for less than the cost of a single video display machine.

Electronic typewriters are best used where appearance is important, and where the length of the documents, the total number of documents, and the requirements for long-term storage are low. There are also some special types of applications, as illustrated in the next chapter.

The principal disadvantage with these machines is obvious: no growth. As in all other phases of office work, storage requirements tend to expand. Careful planning is necessary to be sure that the limits will not be restrictive.

Three last points before we leave electronic typewriters. First, not all machines are alike. Not only do their storage capacities differ, but their formatting features differ as well. These machines should be evaluated as selectively as any other word processor.

Second, because of their built-in memory, there are many things these machines simply cannot do, such as duplicating a page of stored text. If, for example, you wish to store a standard letter and create a second copy for a unique version, you need more sophisticated equipment. It is important to remember that electronic typewriters are a special subset of word processors.

Finally, it should be noted that points one and two do not always apply. Some manufacturers have designed electronic typewriters that can be retrofitted to become full-scale word processors with removable memory and sophisticated editing capabilities. This option is quite attractive. You can start small and still allow for future growth. Independent manufacturers also offer add-on memory devices for some of the more popular machines. Thus, electronic typewriters can play a key role in setting up automated offices.

ABOUT VIDEO DISPLAY TUBES

Before describing the next equipment categories, non-display and display word processors, we must define what a video display tube (VDT) is. Quite simply, it is an electronic screen with an attached keyboard. It looks like a computer terminal such as you might see at any airlines reservation desk. The letters typed on the keyboard appear on the screen. When the image on the screen is satisfactory, it can be stored or transmitted to a printer and produced as a hard copy (on paper) letter.

The principal difference between a VDT and a non-VDT machine is not so much the presence or absence of a screen but how the final copy is produced. In a non-VDT machine, as the typist hits the keys, the information is recorded directly on paper as well as being stored in memory. When a perfect copy is recorded in memory, it is played-out (printed) using the same typewriter element that was used to keyboard (type) the document. (Electronic typewriters also follow this procedure.)

On a VDT machine, the input process (keyboarding) and the output process (printing) use separate devices (the screen and the printer respectively). As a result, keyboarding and printing can occur simultaneously. The productivity gain is significant. A study by a major cereal company demonstrated that it took 11 typists using word processors without VDTs to do the work of seven typists equipped with machines that had them. (With standard electric typewriters, 15 typists were needed to do the same work.)

For the purposes of our discussion, which is categorizing the various levels of machine capability, a non-VDT machine will be considered any word processor that has removable storage media (regardless of the type) and that cannot be used to input and output simultaneously. Thus, machines which offer a single line display are not considered VDT machines, since they do not offer simultaneous typing and printing. Conversely, there are machines with very small displays that do offer this feature and are in another class.

NON-VDT WORD PROCESSORS

Okay, now let's take a closer look at the non-VDT machine. It may look very much like a large version of the electronic typewriter. (See Figure 2.2.) It has the same standard typewriter keyboard, plus some combination of special keys to instruct the machine to center, underline, print, etc. It may have a single line display. Internally, a central processor of some sort will control all these operations.

A non-VDT machine differs from an electronic typewriter in that it will have some place to insert and remove the storage media. It is important to remember that the non-VDT machine may be configured for an electronic typewriter upgraded with removable storage. Some machines incorporate this in the body of the typewriter; others use a separate companion box.

Non-VDT machines, like their electronic typewriter cousins, are relatively low cost word processors. They are particularly effective for repetitive typing and typing with minor additions and deletions of text. These machines do not perform well when entire documents are reorganized. However, because there is no limit to offline (separate from the machine) storage, the machines can be used for long documents that need to be stored for a long time.

Figure 2.2 Non-VDT Word Processor

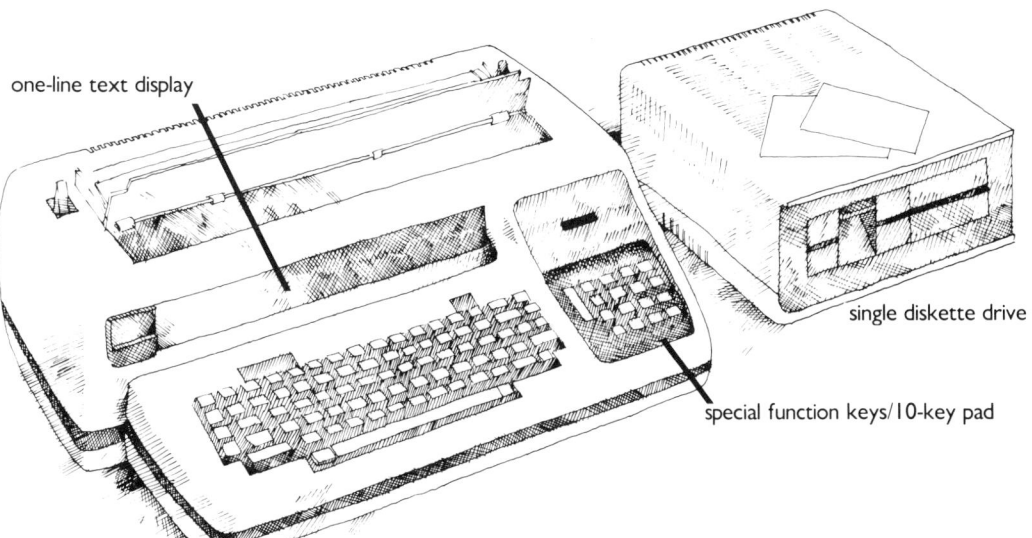

Non-VDT machines, with or without single line displays, are quite sophisticated. They eliminate much of the routine of typing, such as using manual carriage returns, keeping track of margins and lines per page, and filling in the spaces on complex forms. When text is either added or deleted, they automatically adjust the line, paragraph and page, no matter how long the document.

Non-VDT word processors can be used to manage mailing lists, sorting into alphabetical or numerical order as needed. They can also assemble letters from a set of standard paragraphs, merge the letters with a mailing list, and produce a large mailing of personalized letters.

Where non-VDT machines tend to fall short, at least when compared to VDT machines, is in the area of productivity. To print a 20-page draft on a non-display machine ties it up for 20 or 25 minutes. Unless the typist can use this time in some other way, the delay severely cuts into productivity.

VDT WORD PROCESSORS

VDT word processors come in a variety of configurations from stand-alone, self-contained units to shared-resource systems with a number of typing stations (keyboards and displays) linked together electronically.

The stand-alone unit has a VDT (sometimes called a CRT or cathode ray tube), a keyboard with the usual collection of standard and special keys, a printer and a place to insert and remove the storage media. Imbedded somewhere inside is the microprocessor or other computer logic which controls the machine and makes it work. Although the components are usually separate, they can be combined into a single desk-top unit. (See Figure 2.3.)

Depending upon the manufacturer and model, VDT machines vary greatly in capabilities and features. However, all of them have certain advantages in common. As indicated above, they increase productivity by permitting simultaneous operations and by allowing typists to visualize changes and corrections. The displays also work as prompting devices, meaning that typists do not have to memorize complex procedures. This shortens the learning time for new WP typists.

The displays make easier any operation that significantly reorders the text on a page. It is possible to reverse paragraphs, move columns of numbers across a page and even change a word or phrase throughout a document. VDTs are especially useful when a large variety of complex forms is used or when statistical typing is required.

Data processing capabilities are very limited on WP systems without displays. VDT word procesors, however, offer some sophisticated options. These machines offer data processing in one of two ways: either as part of the word processing software provided by the vendor, or as separate software that allows you to run your own programs.

Figure 2.3 VDT Word Processor

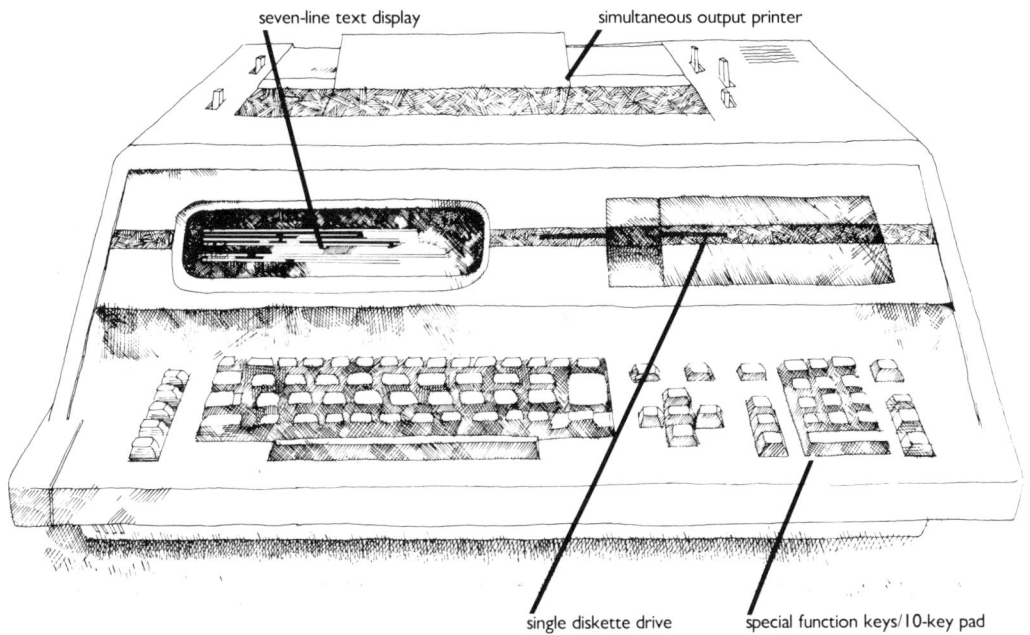

The most commonly used data processing functions incorporated in word processing software are called list processing and math processing. List processing, sometimes called records processing, means sorting keyboarded information in a variety of ways, as well as selecting out important information for reporting or printing. Math processing means using the word processor to perform calculator functions. The easiest way to understand these definitions is to look at some examples.

Let's start with list processing, using the case of a customer file. For each of 500 preferred customers, you might wish to list the company name, contact, title, address, type of business, date of initial purchase, date of last purchase and the quantity or dollar amount. Depending upon the need, you could sort your list in alphabetical order, in postal code order, or by date of most recent purchase. You could also ask for a more selective list, such as all customers who made purchases over a certain dollar amount in the last six months.

The advantages of list processing are many. If you wish to add a name to the middle of the list, it is easy to print out an updated, alphabetized copy. Misfiles are not a problem, since the computer is a better sorter than most people. It is also possible to collect information that would be too time-consuming manually, such as a listing of customers who have not made any recent purchases.

There are some limitations to list processing on WP systems. For very large indexes, such as 5,000 customer names, or where more information about each customer is necessary, the word processor may not have enough sorting speed or capacity. Chapters 9 and 10 explain how to evaluate the potential limitations of a system.

Math processing software, at a minimum, allows you to add, subtract and calculate percentages. Some vendors include a limited financial package which will total columns and calculate negative balances. Others are more sophisticated, allowing you to do virtually anything you can do on a programmable calculator. For a small business, this can simplify invoicing, payroll and accounting without the cost and complexity of a full-scale computer system. Chapter 9 explains how to evaluate math processing in WP software.

SHARED-RESOURCE SYSTEMS

Many large users turn to shared-resource systems to solve their word processing needs. While the initial cost is high, the cost of adding another workstation to the system is relatively low. These systems usually become cost-effective when four or more workstations are involved. They can also be linked to photocomposers and other computers by sophisticated communications networks. (See Figure 2.4.)

Systems share resources in two ways. In a shared-logic system, a single central computer handles all — or most — of the word processing operations. The display workstations cannot function independently; they are called "dumb" terminals.

Other systems distribute the computer logic to the workstations, called "in-

Types of Equipment Available 17

Figure 2.4 Diagram of Shared-Resource System

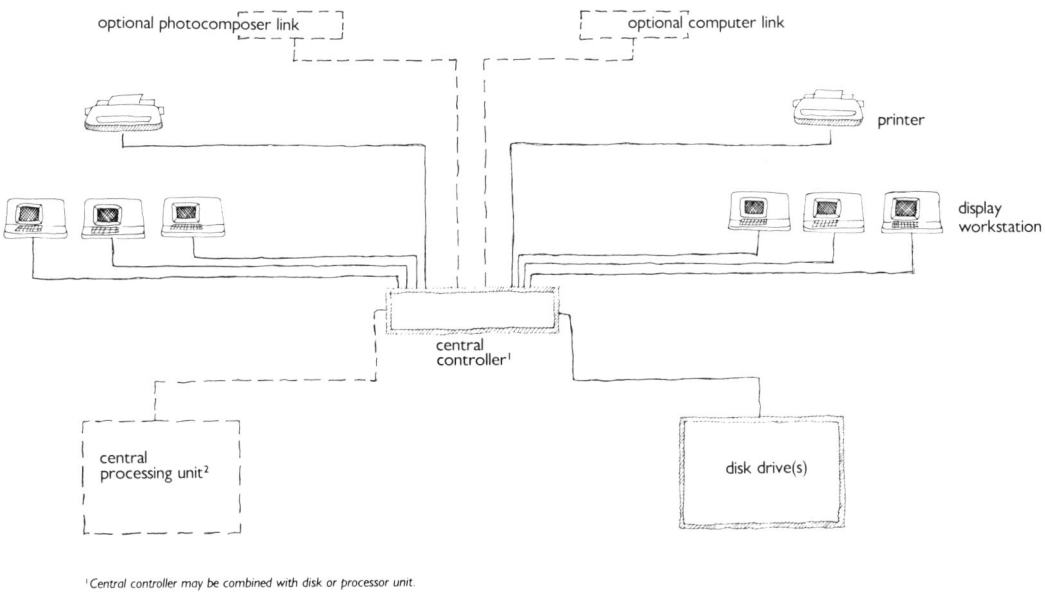

[1] Central controller may be combined with disk or processor unit.
[2] Central processor not used if logic distributed to workstations.

telligent" terminals. However, these terminals do share access to centralized mass storage, usually on hard disks. Thus, they are not completely independent. There is some vulnerability to a failure of the complete system. However, there is less drag on the central processor, which can slow down if too many dumb workstations use it at once.

Hard disks hold up to 40,000 or more pages of text. For very large documents, or when data processing is involved, they are much more efficient file cabinets than the floppy diskettes of most stand-alone units (which hold 125 to 500 pages). This is another of the major advantages of shared-resource systems.

With regard to text editing, the shared-resource systems are not necessarily better than their stand-alone cousins. The workstations look the same, except that there is no place to load a diskette. (See Figure 2.5.) However, the procedures for typing, editing and printing may be identical. In fact, some vendors who make both categories of systems use the same text-editing software for both. The advantage is that stand-alone units can be merged into larger systems as needs grow.

Figure 2.5 Shared-Resource Workstation

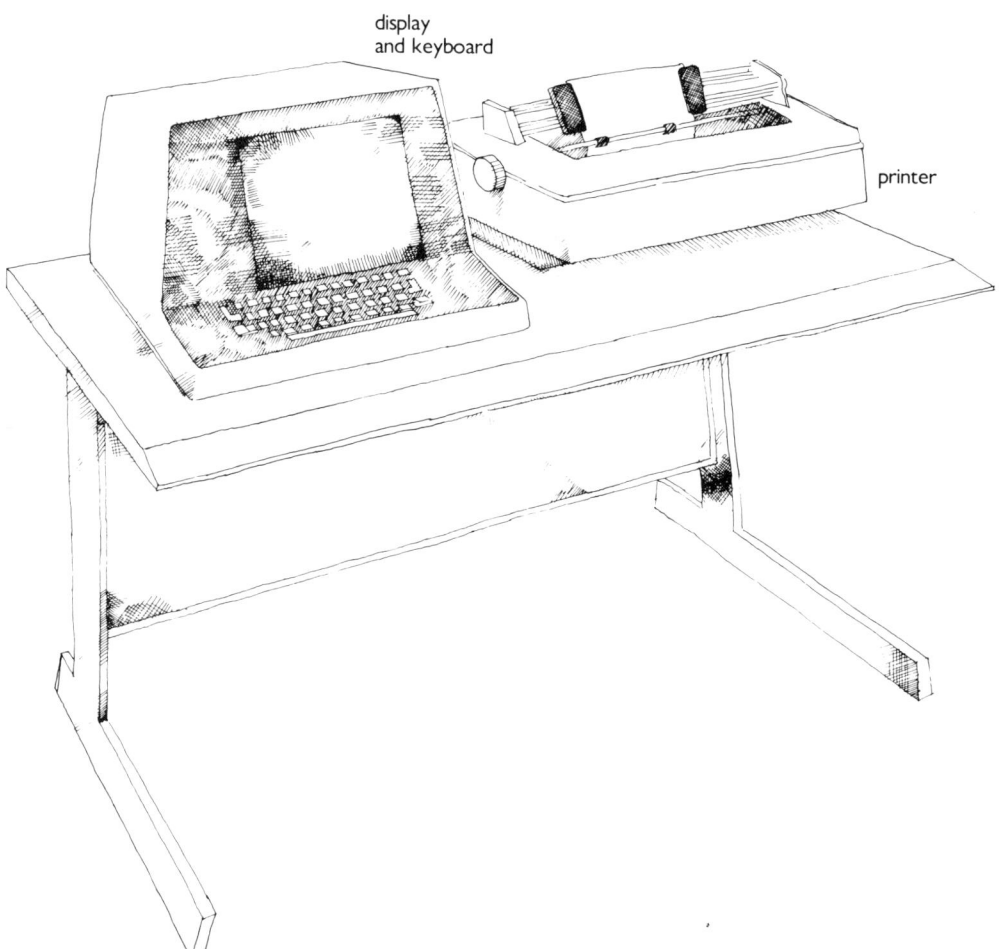

This, then, is the world of hardware and software from which your choices will be made. Understanding the equipment is basic to understanding word processing and its relationship to data processing.

However, as in all things, a little knowledge is dangerous. It is all too easy to start debating the merits of particular machines — after taking in a marathon of demonstrations — before defining what you need. It's like arguing which kind of sedan is best before deciding whether you need a car or a truck. The next step is not to select the right level of machine for your job, but to determine what work you want to do and what features are necessary to do it.

3
Case Studies

Let's take a look at some word processing systems at work, drawing from my own consulting experience. Don't pay too much attention to the types of businesses in the cases below. These are just a few among many possibilities. But do pay attention to the ways in which the equipment is used. The final choice in each case is not the product of chance but of very careful consideration. The cases are arranged from simple to complex. Use them to start thinking about applications in your own business.

ELECTRONIC TYPEWRITER SYSTEMS

Electronic Typewriter Case #1

The client — Marketing Services, Inc. is a small business which develops marketing strategies for other small businesses. The two-person firm also conducts training seminars for business people who wish to develop their own sales and marketing skills. These seminars are often sponsored in-house by large corporations.

The workload — Like many small consulting organizations, Marketing Services is concerned with its image; professionalism is an essential prerequisite. Correspondence, course materials and client marketing reports must have a finished, attractive appearance. Aside from this requirement, however, no significant repetitive or revision applications exist. The average daily workload of 75 lines of typing does not warrant WP support for the occasional retyped letter or report. For a business with a very limited budget, the time saved would not justify the cost of the equipment.

The system — Marketing Systems selected an electronic typewriter that offers right- and left-margin justification and proportional spacing. These two features alone are enough to produce the quality of page the firm requires, and justify the expense of the machine. No storage or display is necessary.

Electronic Typewriter Case #2

The client — Metropolitan Hospital is a 250-bed general care facility, with a medical staff of over 190 affiliated physicians. The hospital has a centralized medical records unit staffed by a supervisor and six secretaries. They transcribe all patient records as dictated by the physicians. The typed reports are routed to the patients' charts, the laboratory, the attending physicians and elsewhere as needed.

The workload — Medical records transcription does not present a typical word processing application. There is no repetitive or revision typing, nor is the appearance of the document important. The unit does, however, produce a high volume of work — about 750 lines of typing per day per typist. (This is about as much original typing as one person can produce in an eight-hour day.) Most of this work is spread over 11 forms, including medical histories, x-ray reports, surgical reports and discharge summaries. At least three carbons are made of each form.

Although the medical records typists are exceptionally good, they do occasionally make mistakes. Most of these are caught as they are made. The problem is correcting all the carbons, which slows the process down considerably. The hospital wants a system that would eliminate this interruption without adding other burdens.

The system — Again, an electronic typewriter fits the bill. A machine with a single line display was chosen. This effectively delays printing of each line until it is completely typed. In other words, as the keys are struck, the characters appear on the display. As the carriage returns, the line is printed and the new line begins to appear in the display. Because the typists catch most errors as they make them, the corrections can be made while the line is still in the display, before it is committed to paper. This means error-free carbons.

Another alternative, of course, would have been to use a VDT. The reports could have been prepared and corrected on the screen and sent to the printer. However, in a case where the only objective is clean carbons, this would have been an extreme solution. Handling the document twice, during input and output, would have actually slowed the typists down. More importantly, the unit was able to buy six electronic typewriters for the cost of one VDT machine.

In addition to producing error-free carbons, the electronic typewriters offer another advantage: the ability to "learn" the format of the forms used by the unit. This eliminates tabbing and other set-up procedures. In addition, the 736-character storage capacity of the typewriter is used to type the official signature blocks that are standard on some of the forms. Altogether, the equipment increased the productivity of the unit by 11%; the supervisor also reported a noticeable increase in morale.

Electronic Typewriter Case #3

The client — The Personnel Department of First City Bank usually receives three or four letters per day requesting employment information. Depending upon the type of applicant, one of four standard letters is usually returned to the correspondent.

The workload — Without word processing, the four one-page letters have to be copied and retyped manually by the departmental secretary. (Preprinted form letters, although less expensive to produce, are considered unacceptable from a public relations standpoint.) In addition, there is a small volume of original correspondence. This consists of short business letters that are rarely revised. About 175 lines per day are typed at this location.

It should be noted that the Personnel Department does have larger typing jobs that require editing and revision. These documents, however, are sent to the bank's centralized word processing center. Where the word processing center does not prove effective is with short letters and personal responses. In both cases, the secretary, who is thoroughly familiar with the work, can prepare the outgoing correspondence from rough notes without doing a draft.

The system — The Personnel Department chose an electronic typewriter with a 15-page non-removable memory. This provides more than enough storage for the standard letters. The additional space is used to create one or two more standard letters and to store and edit the occasional letter the secretary wants to type as a draft first.

The principal gain achieved by this system is increasing the secretary's productivity. Although the typing volume is not large, the other duties of reception, filing and making travel arrangements frequently create a backlog. The addition of the electronic typewriter relieves the backlog with a modest investment, less than the cost of a remote terminal linked to the word processing center. Equally important, although more difficult to document, a highly professional secretary is relieved of the tedium of copying the same letters over and over. Too often this factor is overlooked in office planning, but it is very important to job satisfaction and low personnel turnover rates.

NON-VDT SYSTEM

Non-VDT Case

The client — Computer Personnel is another small firm. There are three principals and a secretary. The firm specializes in recruiting and placing data processing personnel, including managers, systems analysts and programmers. They maintain a large file of positions wanted and another file of personnel available. When a particularly qualified individual becomes available, they may send a number of solicitation letters to prospective employers. Furthermore, for many of their clients, they assist in the development of professional resumes.

The workload — Computer Personnel does not have a large word processing workload. Their daily typing volume fluctuates between 250 and 400 lines. However, there is some repetitive typing, primarily in the multiple solicitation letters they send for special clients. In addition, there is some limited revision typing encountered in the development of professional resumes. Once the clients have an opportunity to review the drafts, they usually suggest minor changes. Likewise, resumes are sometimes reworked slightly to emphasize different points for different prospective employers. The appearance of documents is also considered important, as it reflects upon the professional image of the firm and the client.

More important than the word processing, however, is the list processing application. At any given time, the firm may have a list of 20 or 30 job openings, as well as a client file of 200 or 300 names. Many of these clients are currently employed and, as such, have listed very specific conditions under which they will change employment. Keeping these lists up-to-date and readily available to the recruiting staff is a major activity of the firm's secretary.

The system — Typically, list processing involves a VDT. However, in the case of Computer Personnel, the editing and printing features of such equipment cannot be used effectively. A market search identified one non-VDT system with the list processing capabilities the firm requires. It costs about one-third less than a VDT system with comparable list processing, and for them is a much better value. The firm uses the equipment to maintain current lists. The job openings and personnel available lists are regularly compared. When matches are identified, either through the lists or telephone contacts, letters are prepared to bring the respective parties together. Resumes are updated and revised on short notice to make these presentations as effective as possible.

Computer Personnel cannot justify use of automated equipment in terms of secretarial time saved; there are no backlogs or positions to be eliminated. There is no extra work that can be added. However, the flexibility and faster turnaround time afforded by the equipment boosted the firm's success rate by 9% in the first two months alone. The increase in profitable business more than compensated for the expense.

VDT SYSTEMS

VDT Case #1

The client — Foskett and Ward is a two-attorney law firm specializing in uncontested law. Their practice concentrates on wills, divorces, real estate documents, contracts and bankruptcies. Unlike most law firms, Foskett and Ward charges fixed fees for each type of case. It is for this reason that the firm does not accept contested cases.

The workload — The nature of the work described above lends itself to forms. For almost all types of cases, the lawyers work up interview sheets with the clients. These are designed to merge with various series of standard paragraphs to produce the final legal documents. On typical days, as many as 15 forms may be completed, for an average production of 1,000 lines of typing. About one-third of this is variable information, the rest being standard material. However, there is just enough variation in the arrangement of the standard paragraphs to preclude the use of preprinted forms. Nor would this approach be acceptable to the lawyers in the firm.

The system — Foskett and Ward selected personal computer with WP software for their work. The machine they chose uses diskettes for storage, each one holding up to 125 pages of text. One diskette is dedicated to one or more types of case work, and all possible standard paragraphs are recorded on it. The attorneys have printouts of this prerecorded material. When dictating final documents, they refer to the paragraphs by number, filling in the blanks, and altering the standard material as necessary.

Several points are worth noting here. First, the attorneys can call for the paragraphs in any order. They are not limited to the order of the paragraphs on the diskette. Second, there is no limit to the number of paragraphs that can be stored. The cost of the diskettes (about $5 in 1981) is not significant. Third, because the machine has two diskettes, it is easy for the secretary to duplicate the master paragraphs on a blank diskette. This leaves the masters intact while the copies can be revised. (Having two diskettes is a very useful feature which some of the lowest cost VDT systems do not offer.) Finally, the master diskettes, which contain more than 600 paragraphs and represent a considerable investment in time, are duplicated for off-site security storage.

This machine costs about half of what a true VDT word processor would cost. Its word processing capabilities are also more limited. For instance, after an insertion or deletion, the typist has to instruct the machine manually to reset the right and left margins. Proportional spacing is not available, nor does the machine have any special function keys. Editing tasks must be set up by entering a complex command sequence using the regular typewriter keys in a special shift mode. The machine does, however, offer excellent list processing.

In a case where WP needs are simple and the budget tight, a personal computer can be very practical. If the firm also wants to do any data processing, then the system is even more attractive. (See chapter 10 for more information about office uses for microcomputers.)

VDT Case #2

The client — Nelson and Associates is a seven-member accounting firm. In addition to the principals, there are three secretaries and a part-time bookkeeper. The firm specializes in business accounting; most of its clients are small to mid-size partnerships and corporations. Aside from tax matters, they prepare financial statements, audit reports, and make special reports advising on business decisions on a case-by-case basis.

The workload — Nelson and Associates' work divides into four major categories. The first is tax preparation. Much of this is essentially data processing. It entails collecting information, sorting it into the appropriate categories, tabulating the results, and printing this out in the required format on the appropriate tax forms. Frequently, the same information must be processed a variety of ways to accommodate local and federal tax computations and forms. For this work, the firm leases time from a commercial computer time-sharing service set up specifically for accountants. The cost of updating in-house programs to conform to constant changes in the tax laws would be prohibitive for a firm of this size.

The second major category is research. This is directed to identifying precedent tax law cases, as well as to remaining current on regulations. There are several national reference data bases which offer this information on a subscription basis to users who have their own computer terminals and the appropriate telecommunications.

The third category of work is report preparation. These documents are frequently long, running from 10 to 50 pages or more. They are usually drafted and revised several times, often with extensive changes. Many of the documents involve typing detailed statistical and financial data. Daily workload ranges from 1,500 to 3,500 lines of typing per day. During tax time, no one even counts.

The fourth category is client billing. All professional time is billed by the hour. Different billing rates are established for the various principals of the firm depending on their seniority and expertise. Tax preparation and audit work are also billed at different rates. Finally, there are some items that are billed as fixed costs, such as computer time, copying, long distance phone calls and travel expenses.

The system — Nelson and Associates seeks a system which will handle both its word processing applications and its client billing in a single system. Although the volume of work does not warrant a shared-resource system, they want to be able to share one printer between the VDT typing stations. This permits two typists to have access to the system while costing less than two complete systems. They also require telecommunications capability, so that the word processor can be used as a computer terminal with access to commercial data bases.

Identifying systems to handle the text-editing and research applications is not difficult. Several machines on the market meet the stated requirements, including the necessary telecommunications. Adding in the client billing, however, distinctly narrows the field to systems which include data processing and full programming capability.

Once a decision is reached to use data processing, another must follow closely: whether to write custom programs (or have this done if there are no programmers in-house); or whether to buy commercially-written general programs. The problem with the former is cost in programmers' time and in principals' time to instruct the programmers. The problem with the latter is finding a general commercial program which is a reasonable fit with the firm's specific method of operation.

In this case, the cost differential proved so great — custom programming cost seven times the commercial software price — that the firm elected to modify its methods somewhat to suit the software. In addition, they were able to customize the software they bought, in order to make it a better fit at a reasonable cost. Therefore, selection of the system concentrated not on finding a good word processor but on finding good commercial software. The firm bought the word processor that went with the best client billing program — with good result.

The client billing program is run by the secretaries. The bookkeeper's time is no longer required for this task. The principals keep daily logs of their activities by case, type of activity, and time. These are entered the following morning by the secretary in the same order as they appear in the logs. The machine sorts these random entries into case number order and posts the information to the clients' master records. At the designated billing period, the machine calculates the dollar amounts for professional time and expenses, and prints a bill. This can be detailed or summarized as requested by the client. Balances due, advanced costs, and accounts received are also tracked by machine. (See chapter 10 for more details.)

In addition to the time savings, there are other benefits to the system. With an active client load of 250 cases, the firm cannot afford the time required in a manual system to calculate its outstanding receivables. The new system does this automatically, aging accounts and listing them in order by amounts owing. When clients request invoices on short notice, these can be produced. The master client records are also duplicated once a month and stored off-site.

In the event of fire or vandalism, or even carelessness, the firm can recreate its accounts receivable position with a minimum of difficulty.

Some of the principals initially resisted formalizing their time accounting to the degree required by the computer. However, they were soon won over by the advantages of accurate, current client information. Both secretaries and principals are highly satisfied with the system.

A final note: specialized software markets are developing that may change this firm's dependence on a service bureau for complex tax programs. It is true that one firm cannot afford to maintain up-to-date programs on its own. However, a software company that concentrates on tax preparation packages can afford to do this for a large number of users. The growing number of word processors and personal computers in business and professional firms is creating the necessary customer base. Independent software companies are just beginning to sell and support the kinds of programs that will allow users to do more of their data processing in-house.

VDT Case #3

The client — Environmental Engineering is a large consulting engineering firm specializing in environmental impact assessments. The company has a professional staff of well over 100 people plus 23 secretarial and clerical personnel.

The workload — Environmental impact statements typically run 200 pages or more. Many people may contribute sections to a single report, depending on their various specialties in air and water quality, geology, soil mechanics and so forth. The reports are complex and go through multiple drafts as they are reviewed and integrated.

This kind of typing is often called production typing. It involves long streams of continuous work and does not require close consultation between author and secretary. Several typists may work up different sections simultaneously. In this case, it is also a relatively steady workload of about 16,000 lines of typing per day.

The system — Environmental Engineering has a word processing center to handle production typing. Seven WP typists are required just to keep up with the volume. Both for reasons of cost and to permit shared access to the system's storage, a shared-resource configuration was selected.

A draft line printer and two letter quality character printers are sufficient to handle all typing output. The line printer, at 180 lines per minute, is much faster than the 45 character per second letter quality printers (about 40 to 50 lines per minute). The draft printer is an excellent way to speed preliminary work to authors and supervisors for review. However, it does not produce a clean enough image to be acceptable for final work.

In the case of Environmental Engineering, the shared-resource system replaced obsolete non-VDT magnetic card equipment. The company is now able to discontinue the practice of hiring temporary typists during crunches, an emergency measure which rarely served well. The crunches themselves are better controlled, since substantial backlogs have been eliminated. An internal cost-benefit analysis of the new system confirmed what was already obvious: that the volume of typing, its technical difficulty, the extent of revisions, and the short deadlines simply could not be managed any longer without VDT equipment.

SOME SPECIAL CASES

The cases above are only a sampling of the many ways in which word processing can be effective. There are many other unique applications, dependent largely on the inventiveness of the user.

For example, one municipal court system could not offer civil service salaries high enough to attract qualified typists. The typists they did hire turned non-WP typing into repetitive work by retyping the same letter over to get error-free copy.

The solution was to equip these typists with electronic typewriters having limited-capacity internal memories. In effect, the administrator used electronic typewriters to compensate for inadequate typing skills.

Or let's go back to the firm of Foskett and Ward, the two-member law firm specializing in uncontested cases. They eventually opened a branch office in another section of the same city. As this had been part of their long-range plan, they had carefully selected a personal computer that offered telecommunications compatible with lower level equipment. When the branch office was opened, it was equipped with a remote printer having communications capability. Interview forms prepared at the branch were dictated by phone to the main office secretary. After transcription and typing, the final document was transmitted over phone lines to the branch printer. There it was printed out for the client to sign. Thus, the branch was able to provide full service without having an additional secretary.

In large volume applications, there are equal opportunities for creativity. With the increasing availability of data processing, it is possible to store the information used to create reports on the same machine used to type them. With split screens, it is even possible to view the source information and the report created from it at the same time.

Costs Versus Benefits

In examining the possibilities suggested in this chapter, one or two points should be kept in mind. First, at no point was the gross dollar volume of the business a factor in determining the need for equipment, although it may have had an effect on the acquisition budget.

The real issue was whether or not the cost of the equipment could be offset by other benefits. In some cases, these benefits were directly cost-related, such as reducing a bookkeeper's time, eliminating temporary services, replacing inefficient equipment, or increasing production. In other cases, the benefits were intangible: improving the appearance of correspondence, improving sales performance, or gaining better control over valuable information. Both tangible and intangible benefits can be valid systems justifications when they are well thought out.

The critical factor is to identify those potential benefits correctly, and to select the right equipment to attain them. The next chapters set out a method for deciding whether the work you do can benefit from word processing systems.

4
When To Use WP

In the last chapter, we looked at some problems and saw how they were solved by word processing. The case studies cover most of the basic uses of WP; at least one should have started you thinking about your reasons for turning to WP.

WHAT PROBLEMS CAN WP SOLVE?

The first step is to make sure you should even be thinking about word processing. There are some signals that can tell you if you are on the right track. Some of these relate to people and procedures, others to the kinds of typing your office does. Let's talk about the organizational warning signs first.

Poor Production

In this instance, the typing simply isn't getting out fast enough. For anything under three pages, the turnaround time for a typed document should be about four hours. If it consistently takes longer, there is a problem.

Another clue to poor production is backlogs. The typing may get done on time; it usually takes priority over everything else. However, other essential functions such as filing, ordering of supplies, or processing travel reimbursements may be put off instead. If this is a consistent occurrence, some kind of problem exists.

Unresponsiveness

Unresponsive systems may meet daily work quotas without really meeting users' needs. For example, a consulting engineering firm submits many proposals in its search for contracts. Most competitive bids specify a deadline, and the firm gets its proposals in on time. But that last revision or that last sentence doesn't always get in. It's not just that time is short. It is a perception of too much retyping for a small change. Thus, when the proposal goes out, no one is completely satisfied with it.

Consider another example. A large daily newspaper sells ads to major merchandisers, such as department stores and car dealerships. Their approach is based on market surveys of readers' spending habits for different types of goods. The surveys target appliances, clothes, cars, travel, etc. The marketing staff would like to retype the survey each time it's sent out, highlighting different products for each recipient. This is not practical in a manual system, so it doesn't get done.

A system is unresponsive when authors' needs are not met because of the difficulty involved in retyping a document. Assuming the authors' needs are legitimate, this situation warrants attention.

Poor Quality

Sometimes the authors' revisions aren't responsible for retyping — secretaries and typists make mistakes, too. And sometimes, it seems the problem just won't go away. Regardless of whether poor qualifications or unreasonable demands are at fault, there are a few people who can't type a good letter the first time around. Electronic assistance can help in such a situation.

More importantly, quality relates to the appearance of correspondence. The letter that looks more finished, more polished, competes successfully for attention. For example, preprinted form letters are often used for standard mailings since they are so inexpensive to produce. In personnel or sales situations, however, their impact is decidedly negative. People have come to expect the finished look that goes with word processing. In fact, a professional fundraiser found that a letter produced using WP, generated several times the net return of a preprinted form letter.

Excessive Record Keeping

This is a difficult problem to isolate, let alone resolve. It gets to the very root of how work is done in an office. Typically, it relates more to data processing than word processing. However, when properly identified, some innovative solutions using WP equipment can be found.

By way of definition, let's consider some examples. The first is a local prosecutor's office. The domestic relations section monitors 5,500 child support cases. This means tracking social worker visits, updating addresses, scheduling hearings and reporting on all activities and overdue payments.

When a social worker's report is received, the date is posted in the case file. A notice is sent to the attorney and the other parent. When an address is changed, the case file is updated and notices are sent to all parties. Each attorney maintains a list of clients by scheduled hearing date. Postponements are requested and new schedules must be typed.

The real work, however, occurs at the end of the month: how many cases were opened, closed, had social worker reports, went to trial, or were delinquent? When it comes time to prepare the monthly reports, all other work shuts down for at least one day. This kind of repetitive record keeping is a good candidate for automation. The fact that so much of it is tied to producing notices, routine letters and reports suggests an enhanced word processing system might be the answer.

All of these problems are warning signals that something is wrong. These kinds of situations are frequently improved by using WP. But not always. Adding automation to a poorly designed office procedure will only make it worse. It is always wise to streamline operations manually first. Look at office organization, document flow, forms design and filing procedures. When you are satisfied that these areas are functioning well, and you still have problems, it's time to take a closer look at automation.

There are two things word processing does really well: store text and reformat text. With the addition of some computer programs, it can also maintain the files that are used to create the typed letters and reports. The next step, then, is to examine the office's typing to see if these kinds of work are being done. If they are, then we will also want to know how much.

We looked at some equipment and some typical uses in chapters 2 and 3. Now let's look at the specific kinds of work that are suited to WP.

WHAT IS WP TYPING?

There are three basic categories of WP typing: special format typing, repetitive typing and revision typing. Record keeping and math computations can also be considered. Work that can be handled using standard WP software is described here. (For anything more complex, see chapter 10.) The principal applications for which WP should be considered are as follows.

Special Format Original Typing

Typically, this is correspondence or short reports, each unique and each typed only once. For example, an executive office might want the ability to justify right and left margins, use proportional spacing, or prepare dual columns of text. The last feature lets you print an English and French version very neatly side by side. This kind of typing takes full advantage of the *format* capabilities of WP, which control the *appearance* of the product. Storage of information may not be necessary.

Repetitive Typing

This usually includes standard letters which are used over and over again. Only the name and a small amount of information changes each time. Repetitive typing also refers to the use of standard paragraphs or sets of information (such as market research statistics). These are selected and put together in a variety of ways to suit specific purposes.

Repetitive typing also refers to the same format being used over and over, such as on standard forms. Anyone who has ever typed a form knows how time-consuming it is to align tabs and spaces. It's especially frustrating when you use the same form over and over again. Even a very limited word processor can remember the format for you, so that advancing from item to item is accomplished with a single keystroke.

Revision Typing

This includes letters, reports and other documents that are drafted, edited, and retyped. Frequently, text is inserted or deleted. Whole paragraphs may be reordered. Columns of numbers may be shifted across a page to make room for the current month's figures. Large catalogues or procedures manuals may be updated. These tasks involve keyboarding some new lines, while reusing any part of the previous version that did not change.

Some typing is so difficult that it is automatically considered revision typing. Examples are columnar and other statistical typing, equations and highly technical information. The complexity of these materials makes it poor practice to risk a manual retype. This is true even if the only changes are to correct typing errors.

List Processing

This term refers to the kinds of record keeping and indexing operations that can be handled using the standard software that comes with most word processors. Some equipment vendors also refer to these operations as records management.

Let's look at another example, going back to the hospital with 190 doctors on its staff. The physicians work in six separate departments. Each doctor has a regular schedule, an emergency room schedule and a continuing medical training schedule. The entire roster of doctors is sometimes sorted in alphabetical order, sometimes by department, and sometimes by scheduled day off. Special lists of which doctors are certified and by which board are also prepared.

In the manual system, the staff secretary maintains 20 separate lists to meet all the information requests. Using WP, one complete record is maintained for each doctor. It contains 20 separate data elements, or fields of information, about each doctor. There are now 190 *records,* each divided into 20 *fields.* Each field contains a fixed number of *characters* (letters, numbers, punctuation and spaces). For instance, 28 characters are set aside for each doctor's name. The full record thus contains 250 characters spread over the 20 fields.

Once the list is set up, it can be used two ways. The first is simply to sort the list into a revised order. For example, you can change it from postal code order to alphabetical order. In a multi-level sort, you can sort the doctors in order by department, and within each department in alphabetical order. This is a two-level sort. Six- and even ten-level sorts are possible.

The other way the list is used is to extract only those records that meet certain search criteria, called qualifiers. For example, you can ask the system to list all the doctors who have served for more than five years and who have expressed an interest in being department heads. This is a two-level select (sometimes called extract). Multi-level extracts with up to six or eight qualifiers at a time are possible.

To select a record, the system matches the information you specify against the information in the record. It can test for greater than, and/or equal to, and/or less than. This kind of search is called Boolean logic. The full record, or only those fields which are of special interest, can then be printed.

List processing that can be done without special programming can usually be expressed in the terms described above. If you think you have an application, try to reduce it to quantitative terms: how many records, how many fields, how many characters per field? Describe the typical sorting and extracting which you will need to do. If you have trouble arranging your information this way, it's probably not a good application. Once you have this quantitative description of your file, vendors can tell you whether or not their standard software can handle it. If not, you still have the option of considering data processing (see chapter 10).

Math Processing

Many word processors offer math capabilities. At a low level, these machines can add up columns or calculate percentages. The more sophisticated machines can tabulate up to 10 intermediate subtotals and carry them to a final page for a grand total. Top of the line machines can do almost anything a programmable calculator can do. They even can remember a simple series of steps to perform the same calculation over and over.

Small businesses frequently take advantage of this feature for such routine calculations as invoicing or expense accounting. Larger firms often install equipment with these capabilities in their finance and accounting offices. The equipment checks column totals, updates year-to-date expenditure reports, and even calculates taxes and sales commissions.

Finding good applications in your business takes creativity and some digging. But the payoff is worth the effort. The next step is to describe your work in the terms outlined in this chapter.

5

Defining Your Workload

Most organizations which are considering WP equipment do some kind of an analysis or study. The reason for doing a WP study is simple: to identify the kind and amount of WP typing that needs to be done. The study process itself can range from the simple to the complex, depending largely on the complexity of the organization itself. Not surprisingly, a two-person law office is easier to survey than a 135-member engineering firm.

As a general rule, the more rigorous the study, the more precise the final systems design will be. In a large organization, some kind of quantitative analysis is essential. In a small business, you can be somewhat more subjective.

GETTING STARTED

Whatever your approach to analyzing your needs, there are some important first steps. In a large organizaton, they are essential. A small business will also benefit from their discipline. The purpose is to reduce the office's natural resistance to change by removing as much mystery from WP as early as possible.

When you change the way an office does its work, you need to make sure the office will follow your lead. It is not enough to have a clear picture of the workload and to know that WP will solve all your problems. You also need to have the full support of both management *and* staff. The preliminary steps outlined below will smooth the way.

Define Objectives

Decide in advance what benefits you expect or will accept. Be very wary of committing yourself to dollar savings as the sole criterion for justifying the cost of your new system. You may find at the conclusion that there is a valid case for WP in your company. You may be able to solve many of the problems we talked about in the last chapter. But you may find that so doing will cost you some money. Think your objectives through carefully, and then stick to them.

Obtain Management Support

No doubt you have heard that before, but it's important. Make sure management understands and is committed to the same objectives. Otherwise, at the end, they may reject any proposal that doesn't cut secretarial staffing.

Assemble the Survey Team

You basically have three choices: an in-house team, consultants, or vendors. Their relative merits are these:

In-House Study Team

Advantages: Knows the organization. Builds commitment and expertise in-house. Low cost (assuming personnel time is available.).

Disadvantages: May have biases which make it difficult to be objective. Experience limited to single organization. Not always expert in WP marketplace and systems analysis and design.

Comments: If you set up an in-house study team, make sure all users are represented: management, personnel and data processing staffs; authors and secretaries. Designate a lead, but keep everyone involved.

Consultant

Advantages: Knows WP, especially if you find a good one. Knows other organizations. Can save you from reinventing others' mistakes. Has a tested study methodology.

Disadvantages: Expensive. Has to learn your organization.

Comments: Look for someone who will work with your staff, who will develop in-house skills. Obtain a specific written proposal and check references carefully. A good consultant will be willing to support your in-house team as an expert resource.

Vendor

Advantages: No cost. Often quite knowledgeable in the field.

Disadvantages: Obvious biases. Can create a sense of obligation, even if not deliberate.

Comments: Ask the vendor to share collected data with you, not just conclusions. Be wary of vendors who use "industry standards" to decide on the right number of machines. The industry tends to be theirs, not yours.

Develop a Work Plan

First, define your scope of investigation. Don't bite off too much at once. Two or three smaller studies are easier to manage than one large one. Otherwise, you waste too much time on coordination. It is also better to start small until you are very sure of your survey methods. There are two parts to a good work plan:

(a) *Office orientation:* Collect organization charts, mission statements, personnel lists, inventories of current WP equipment and costs, and floor plans. Figure out who will be studied, and in what order. Learn as much about the office as you can.

(b) *Survey methodology:* Determine your study methodology. Details of how to conduct document samples, workload measurement and personal interviews are discussed in the rest of this chapter. At this point, you need to pick the specific tools you will use and get them ready. If you are going to require extra personnel or data processing to tabulate the results of your study, plan for this now.

Inform All Employees

Before you get started, let everyone know what you are doing. Make sure they understand the objectives of your study, who will be involved and what will be required of them. Provide a contact who can answer questions with sensitivity, in confidence if necessary. Provide a formal presentation on word processing. Include a demonstration or movie if you can. There is a direct correlation between the amount of cooperation received and the amount of mystery that is removed from WP. Don't communicate by rumor.

COMPONENTS OF THE STUDY

There are three components to a word processing study: a document sample, a workload measurement and a staffing review. In this chapter we will describe each of the three components. For each one, we will define an objective — what it is we are looking for — and describe two methods for attaining that objective. The first is a shortcut approach, appropriate for a small office or where the answers to your study questions are fairly clear. The second method is a complete and objective study methodology, including detailed work measurement. You may mix and match to tailor the kind of study that best fits your own organization. There are no hard and fast rules. Just be sure to keep your study objectives clearly in mind.

The Document Sample

The document sample answers the question: "What kinds of WP typing do we do?" Thus, it reviews at least one example of every document that fits the descriptive categories outlined in chapter 4. The purpose is to establish the mix of repetitive, revision and other typing. This, in turn, determines the level or levels of equipment that will be required. For instance, a concentration of repetitive typing might indicate a blind machine. High volumes of revision point to the need for a VDT.

. . . What kind of typing do we do?

Collecting a document sample will not tell you everything you need to know about your applications. The secretary may forget to submit something, or the work may not occur during the study period. List processing and math applications may not show up as typing workload at all. Don't hesitate to poke around the office. Look into a few file folders. Ask about monthly reports, cross-indexes, card files. Do this even if you think you know your business backwards and forwards. The answers may surprise you.

Shortcut via Questionnaires

Have all personnel who do typing collect samples of their work. Develop a structured questionnaire rather than asking for one of everything. The questionnaire should identify the kinds of things you are looking for, arranged according to the categories of WP work discussed in the last chapter. Explain the categories using examples that relate to your business. Have respondents submit one sample of each document that fits your definitions. For each sample they submit, ask respondents to answer these basic questions:

(a) For repetitive typing: How often is it typed? Is the whole document reproduced or just certain paragraphs? How many documents at a time? How long on the average?

(b) For revision typing: How often? What percent revised? How many times? Average length?

(c) For list processing and math applications, have the study participants describe and quantify them as best they can. Go back and take a look at the promising ones.

Formal Study

The most reliable method for conducting work samples is to collect a copy of everything that is typed over a certain period of time. Usually, this is done in conjunction with a work measurement study as described in the next section. In this case, you sort the output into the appropriate categories.

Ten working days seems to be the most appropriate period for collecting the sample. Choose your survey time carefully. Peaks and valleys distort the results. Yet it is certainly important to plan for them. One option is to break up your survey period into two parts. Sample a peak period for one week and a normal or slack period the other week.

It is not necessary to plan your survey around personal schedules. A certain amount of sick leave and vacation time will always occur. Only unusual absences disqualify a study period. If you regularly employ temporary help for typing, make sure their work is included in the survey.

Work Measurement Study

The work measurement study answers the question, "How much typing do we do?" Again, there are two ways of getting at the answer.

. . . How much typing do we do?

Shortcut via Questionnaires

Working from the questionnaires and collected samples, estimate how much WP typing is done. Estimate the number of lines per day of original, repetitive and revision typing. Start by typist and work up to the entire office.

Formal Study

During the two week document survey, ask the typists to answer certain questions about *every* document they type. A structured approach is best. Formulate questions which address your concerns about equipment. For instance, if you are considering machine dictation systems, you will want to identify all short documents that are being handwritten.

If you are producing long documents and lots of copies, you might want to keep track of the volume. High-speed printers and intelligent copiers might be practical for your application. The items of information most commonly collected are listed below.

(a) Respondent: Name and organization

(b) Input: Longhand, shorthand, or machine dictated? Copied from other typewritten material? Composed by the typist?

(c) Output: First final? First draft? Revised document? How many times revised? What percent changed? Repetitive document?

(d) Format: Form or text?

(e) Special handling: Machine copies made? How many sets? Internal or external distribution? Statistical typing?

(f) Workload measures: Number of pages typed? Number of lines?

Arrange your questions in a daily typing log or other easy-to-use data collection form. Don't forget to leave space for the date of each day's log at the top. Set up the form so that the secretary can fill in a line of information for each document typed. This will also simplify tabulating the results. If you are planning to use data processing, take this into account in designing your form. Make sure you coordinate your plans with your data processing support.

Introduce the data collection procedure at special training sessions. Distribute written instructions for the typing logs. The participants can refer to these during the survey. (These same instructions will help the data processing staff to tabulate the survey results.) It usually helps to take a few sample documents to the session. The correct logging of these should be explained to the group. Ask the typists to attach a copy of everything they type to their daily log, and in the same order as the entries in the log.

Document surveys are best started mid-week. The training can be done in one afternoon and the survey begun the following morning. Monday morning starts are too rushed. Besides, no one carries a Friday afternoon training session over to Monday morning.

Collect the logs daily. Review them to make sure they are accurately and completely filled out. If a blank log is submitted, note whether the typist was absent or simply did not do any typing that day. This will help you assess overall staffing needs.

No survey is ever completely representative. There is always some major task that does not occur during the scheduled period. Ask participants to include samples of these documents in their submissions. This work should not be recorded on the daily typing logs. An explanation of what the job is, how long or complex it is and how often it is done should be annotated on the sample.

At the conclusion of the survey, you will want to get some feedback as to how representative the measured workload really was. Either by questionnaire or interview, ask the participants the following questions:

(a) Backlogs: What typing was backlogged at the beginning of the survey? At the end? What about other work, such as filing?

(b) Volume: Was the typing during this period normal, heavy, or light? What about other work? By how much was it off?

Staffing Review

The traditional justification for adding WP equipment has been subtracting people. In the next chapter, we will talk about this and other methods of justification in detail. Before you start asking whether WP will allow you to reduce staff, however, you should first ask whether you are properly staffed to begin with. Although this book will not attempt to tell you everything about staffing your office, it can help you plan for WP-related changes.

There is secretarial work in your office that has nothing to do with typing. WP people call it administrative support, or AS for short. When you change the way some of the typing or office record keeping is done, administrative work is affected as well. At the very least, the typing will take less time. There may be significant redistribution of work among offices.

Deciding how to use this time is the reason for doing an administrative support study. It identifies authors' needs, administrative workload volume, problems and bottlenecks.

One of the key issues is whether support personnel can assume more administrative work once they are equipped with word processing. The entire process is designed to identify all the necessary adjustments in the office caused by implementation of WP.

A shortcut and several formal methods for getting at staffing needs are discussed below. However, it is not necessarily an either/or process. The shortcut method is more subjective. It presumes that if you ask the right questions, you can collect enough information to make good decisions. In many, many organizations, this is true. Common sense should not be ruled out. Personal questionnaires or interviews may tell you all you need to know.

There are, however, some formal methods of data collection. These are more objective, although they are subject to a certain amount of distortion. Any of these methods is valid, depending upon the nature of the organization and what you are trying to do.

Formal studies are very useful if you need to establish priorities among several offices competing for a limited budget. They are less useful for obtaining an absolute measure of exactly how much administrative work is being done. Think carefully about what information you will need to make decisions. Choose whichever tools will best help you collect it.

Shortcut via Questionnaires

Listed below are sample questions for authors and secretaries. No doubt, you will have some of your own. Organize your questions to bring a logical structure to your analysis. Personal interviews yield the most informative answers. Distribution of written questionnaires is acceptable.

Questions for authors:

(a) Current level of AS support: Adequate? Secretary available when needed? Filing and information retrieval OK? Any specific administrative problems? Bottlenecks? Author doing any clerical work?

(b) Current AS workload: What AS support tasks need doing? What paraprofessional tasks? Can more work be delegated?

(c) Current typing workload: What turnaround time required? How much is confidential? What kind of typing required? Printing and distribution requirements? Production problems?

(d) Future workload: Predicted growth or reorganization? Recurring peaks and valleys?

Questions for secretaries:

(a) Major tasks performed: Listed in order from most to least time consuming. (You may suggest a list, or allow respondents to create their own.)

(b) Authors supported: How many? Satisfactory arrangement?

(c) Equipment needs: Transcribers, computers, word processors available? Needed? Adequate access?

(d) Special tasks: Special training or skills required? Knowledge of office procedures required? Independent paraprofessional responsibilities?

(e) Job assessment: Problems or bottlenecks identified? Preferred tasks? Tasks liked least? Able to keep pace with work? Suggestions for improvement?

Formal Study

There are at least two ways to measure administrative workload. Both involve a statistical sample. The first is based on randomly scheduled observations of what typists and other support personnel are doing. The second asks them to keep track of their time for you.

Observation sampling — requires a member of the survey team to sample and note what tasks are being performed by whom at selected times during the day. If you make enough observations of all staff activities over a period of time, you can determine how much time is devoted to each activity. The number of observations required can be computed for your organization by anyone with a statistical background.

There are two problems with this kind of sample. First of all, the activity being performed is not always obvious to the observer. Is this a personal call or a business call? Does the empty desk mean a coffee break or a messenger errand? Aside from problems of accuracy, people are not especially fond of being watched.

The biggest problem, however, is cost. Someone has to make the observations, often 8 or 10 times a day. Unless there is some strong requirement for an accurate measure, this is not a good use of survey team time.

Self-measurement — requires that the participants report their time by type of activity. Usually, this is done over the period of the work measurement study. When tabulated, the results are a statistical summary of daily activities. The principle is the same as for the random observation method described above.

In practice, of course, the answers are distorted. No one ever works less than eight solid hours per day. Some distortion is deliberate, of course, to disguise wasted time. And some simply reflects the fact that participants find it boring to note their tasks every five minutes or so. There is too much happening, too much work to be done. So they tend to summarize just before the forms are collected. Considering that they are also filling out daily typing logs, who can blame them?

When your study is complete, you will have a clear idea of your office's typing and other workload. The next step is to match it up with the right WP equipment and staffing.

6

Interpreting the Results of the Study

The document sample and work measurement results will provide most of your answers about WP equipment. You will know what you should have. Then comes the process of justifying the system; it tells you what you can have. Often, the two answers are the same. But sometimes a scaled-down design makes more sense. This is where the staffing level analysis becomes important.

Before we begin, there is one more rule. It is that there are no fixed rules. WP and AS are part of a larger picture that includes people, priorities and change. It is not possible to reduce the entire operation to workload statistics. There is no absolute standard that says the same results *always* mean the same thing.

The study process is an attempt to bring some order to our understanding of a complex organization. Work measurement in particular is an excellent tool. But it does not preclude using good judgment. Keep your original objectives in mind and don't be tempted to modify them as you go along. Above all, when you have completed your systems design, the best test is still: "Does it make sense?"

WHAT THE DOCUMENT SAMPLE TELLS YOU

Use the document sample to figure out what level or levels of WP systems you should be looking at. Begin by organizing the sample according to the basic categories of WP work outlined in chapter 4.

If you have done a formal work measurement, this task will be easier. The tabulated results will tell you whether you have repetitive, revision, forms, statistical, or other typing. The document sample simply provides depth to the statistical overview. If you have not done a work measurement study, the document sample is your primary source of information.

Either way, you will want to work up a list of what kinds of applications you have and what category they fall into. The earlier chapters in this book should give you some good ideas. But let's throw in a few more just to make the definitions really clear.

Repetitive Typing

This includes standard documents, whether the entire text is reused or just various sections are revised. This includes personnel correspondence, position descriptions, routine notices, promotional mailings and even reports. Frequently, a regular report carries much of the same information from month to month. A budget report that lists year-to-date expenditures against the budgeted amount is a good example.

Frequently typed forms are also an excellent application. Wills, contracts, other legal documents, proposals, specifications, directories and collective bargaining agreements also can fit here.

As an example, an equal employment opportunity agency writes up complaints as part of the investigative process. Since the complaints are all made under the same laws, the writeups tend to follow certain patterns. The investigators have created a library of standard paragraphs covering most situations. Each has designated blanks for specific information. The investigators request the paragraphs by number, and dictate the missing information for each one. A good use of equipment, but still basically repetitive typing.

As a general rule, repetitive typing lends itself to electronic typewriters or non-display machines. Repetitive typing does not require much machine sophistication. It is also true that the machine is not available for other uses during printout. There are non-display machines equipped with automatic paper feeds. These machines can handle a large printing job while the typist does some other non-typing task. This is sort of a poor man's version of simultaneous input and output.

The more complex the repetitive application, the more sophisticated the equipment will have to be. If the principal use is to store the setup of a standard form, an electric typewriter will do. Form letters may require an electronic typewriter with some additional storage or a blind machine with removable memory. Working with standard paragraphs can be done on a blind machine. However, if the assembled documents are complex, or if much non-standard material is to be added, a VDT may be necessary.

Revision Typing

Light revision involves changing less than 10% of a document. Usually, there is one draft prior to final. If the volume is also light, this kind of revision can be handled on non-display equipment. The test is the personnel time lost because there is no simultaneous input and output. If the application involves occasional changes to letters, the personnel time lost will not be great. If 30-page reports are standard fare, blind equipment is not efficient.

Heavy revision typing involves changing 10% to 50% of a document. (If more than 50% is changed, it is usually easier to start over.) Documents may be revised one or several times. This kind of work is best done using display equipment.

Another application best handled on a VDT machine is complex document assemblies. If the library of paragraphs is extensive, the typist may want to preview the choices and the current version before committing to print. Some systems have a split screen to permit simultaneous viewing of the master and the current version. For contracts and legal work, this is very useful.

Virtually all editing functions require a VDT. The screen allows the WP typist to see and experiment with text prior to printing. In a non-display system, each change must be checked by printing out. This is too slow if editing is a regular activity. Some features, such as automatic outline and index generation, are so complex they are only offered on display equipment.

Other editing features on VDT machines simplify columnar and scientific typing. For example, a long set of numbers can be typed in a single column without regard to placement. At the end, tab settings are established for as many columns as the typist wants. The system automatically distributes the numbers evenly among them. Alphabetical lists can also be handled this way. Afterwards, the typist can switch, delete, or move whole columns about the page at will.

Statistical typing, because of its complexity and accuracy, is recommended for VDT equipment. VDT systems also handle footnotes and scientific notation well. They can number footnotes automatically and control the placement of reference marks and footnotes on the same page.

VDTs are not perfect, of course. One of their hangups is typing equations. Scientific notation requiring Greek letters must be handled with special printers. These permit more than one character set (alphabet) to be used at the same time. However, if there are extensive subscripts and superscripts as well, there can be problems. What you see on the screen may not be what you get. If you work with equations, ask for a complete demonstration of the typing cycle from input to printing.

In short, revision typing refers to text changes and editing. Sophisticated format controls are important, too. If your workload fits in the pigeonholes described above, VDT equipment is probably what you should be looking for.

List Processing

List processing, as defined in the previous chapter, involves setting up records of information which can be sorted and printed in a variety of ways. Most list processing applications are done on VDT equipment. There are also blind machines that do sorting and selecting. However, offices where the work involves list processing usually do revision and editing work as well. Therefore, a VDT makes the most sense. The screen enables the typist to experiment with the format before printing the selected records.

As indicated in the previous chapter, list processing applications (or files) must be reduced to quantitative terms: how many records, how many fields, and how many characters? How long will it take to sort the entire file? How long to select and print 50% of the records in a multilevel sort?

The vendors can help you with the time questions. The speed varies from machine to machine. You will have to decide if the word processor method looks too cumbersome or too slow. If so, you will need to evaluate expanded data processing capability. This can be part of your WP system, or perhaps a separate computer entirely. Chapter 10 explains how to make this choice.

Math Processing

Columnar typing, decimal alignment and even adding column totals are not true math applications. These features are more related to formatting than to computation. The ability to total a column is usually a proofreading aid. The typist can cross-check a typed total with the one in the author's draft.

True math typing, therefore, involves more extensive computation. For example, a western wood products company uses rail, trucks and ships to move its products. Comparative rate schedules are prepared for distribution to the mills. The charts are complex, since rates vary with volume, weight and distance. Sometimes a shipper announces an across-the-board 10% increase in rates. The firm's WP system calculates the new rates in each category and prints the revised schedules.

Math software may be used to do routine calculations in reports. For example, a monthly expenditure report may calculate the actual expenditures to date as a percent of the budgeted amount. The operator only enters the figures; the machine computes the percentages.

Applications such as these are suitable for display equipment. At some point, of course, you must ask yourself whether a WP system is the right solution to a math problem.

By now, you should have a good list of WP applications in your business. You should also have a level of equipment in mind. Or maybe a combination of different machines is what you need. But you still aren't sure how many machines. That's the next step in the process.

WHAT WORK MEASUREMENT TELLS YOU

Workload statistics — whether measured or estimated — tell you the number of lines of typing you do per day. By dividing this figure by the number of lines per day that a typist can produce, you know how many typists you need to do your work. This is the same as knowing how many machines you need, since there is a one-to-one relationship between typists and machines.

In a small organization, you may not need work measurement to tell you how many machines you should have. Your budget tells you quite clearly that one will be plenty. The line counts are still useful, however, as a measure of the value you will get from that single machine. For instance, your typist may average 500 lines per day. Even a blind word processor can easily handle two or three times that amount. WP equipment will be difficult to justify in such a case.

In a large organization, the workload statistics give you a rational basis for evaluating competing priorities. It is rare that all offices' requirements are equal and that there is enough money to equip everyone. Without workload measures, it is difficult to make unbiased choices and to separate equipment decisions from organizational politics. With measures, it is easier to be fair, to match resources and requirements accurately, and to have some confidence that you will receive value for your investment.

Production Factors

Your WP study tells you how many lines per day your typists are producing now. The tables below tell you how many lines they can be expected to produce using WP equipment. Table 6.1 presumes a fairly even mix of original, repetitive and revision typing. It also takes into account different levels of skill and different types of equipment.

Table 6.1 Daily Production Values (in lines per day)

	Excellent	Good	Average
Electric/electronic typewriter	750+	500-750	250-500
Non-display word processor	1500+	1100-1500	700-1100
Display word processor	2200+	1600-2200	1000-1600

Table 6.2 provides weighting factors. It recognizes that not all lines of typing are equal. For instance, typing a page of equations is much slower than printing a one-page repetitive letter. If your workload is exceptionally skewed in favor of statistical work or repetitive letters, you can use the weighting factors to recompute your line counts. If you do use them, divide the weighted counts by the excellent production values to estimate daily output. Weighting precludes using lower daily figures.

Table 6.2 Weighting Factors
(1 typed line = how many weighted lines)

Repetitive typing and printing	1
Forms* typing	1
Original lines	1.5
Statistical lines	2
Up to 10% revision lines	1.1
Up to 20% revision lines	1.2
Up to 30% revision lines	1.3
Up to 40% revision lines	1.4
Up to 50% revision lines	1.5

*A form line takes longer to set up, but is usually shorter.

Comparing the unweighted and weighted results can help you with borderline decisions. If the unweighted values indicate you need 2.5 WP typists, the weighting factors can help you decide whether to go with two or three. For the most part, you can ignore them while doing your study. However, if you plan to charge your WP customers for services by the line, you will want to consider them again when setting your rates.

Both Tables 6.1 and 6.2 presume full-time typing. If a typist is producing 250 lines of typing per day, this does not necessarily mean a below average employee. Any number of other duties may account for the low typing volume.

However, no matter how good the person, if a typist is producing 250 lines per day now, don't expect 2,000 lines per day with VDT equipment — unless some other workload adjustments are made. Be sure to take this into account in planning for the number of machines you will need.

Let's take a look at two examples of how the tables are used. In the first, we will work with unweighted line counts only. In the second, we will see how weighting can assist in the decision process.

Case #1: City Newspaper Office

The business office of a major metropolitan paper surveyed its typing workload. The results indicated an average output of 9,450 lines per day, including original, repetitive, and revision work. Fourteen typists participated; individual output averaged 675 lines per day. This equates to a full-time typing workload for each person.

Using a simple ratio, anticipated production levels were calculated for VDT and non-VDT word processors, as follows:

Non-VDT

$$\frac{675 \text{ lines/day (current level)}}{750 \text{ lines/day (current maximum)}} = \frac{x \text{ lines/day (anticipated level)}}{1{,}500 \text{ lines/day (maximum possible)}}$$

VDT

$$\frac{675 \text{ lines/day (current level)}}{750 \text{ lines/day (current maximum)}} = \frac{x \text{ lines/day (anticipated level)}}{2{,}200 \text{ lines/day (maximum possible)}}$$

The results indicate anticipated levels of 1,350 and 2,000 lines per day for non-VDT and VDT word processors respectively. These figures, in turn, are used to compute the number of word processors required, as follows:

Non-VDT

$$\frac{9{,}450 \text{ actual lines/day}}{1{,}350 \text{ anticipated lines per person}} = 7 \text{ full-time typists}$$

VDT

$$\frac{9{,}450 \text{ actual lines/day}}{2{,}000 \text{ anticipated lines per person}} = 4.75 \text{ full-time typists}$$

The number of WP typists required is calculated both ways because the survey indicates that different offices can benefit from different levels of word processors. For example, the personnel office does not need a display, while the finance group most certainly does. The labor relations office has the appropriate workload for a VDT, but not enough volume. However, its geographical separation in another building precludes sharing. A non-VDT machine is a good compromise. In all, three stand-alone VDT word processors and three non-VDT machines were selected. Two of the VDT workstations were able to share a single printer between them.

There are a couple of points worth noting here. First, some compromises were made to accommodate a decentralized work force. Unfortunately, people and machines come in whole numbers; it is not possible to have 4.75 VDT machines. But creativity was applied, taking up the slack with less expensive machines and sharing printers when possible.

Second, the number of full-time typists dropped from 14 (old system) to 6 (new system). The newspaper's job is not done yet: staffing and work assignments must be adjusted to complement the change.

Finally, one last comment for you TV fans. The newspaper does have an online text editing system for reporters. It is also used to set up the classified ads, something they don't tell you on "Lou Grant." The operation of the equipment, therefore, is very different. For instance, it formats line by line, whereas a WP typist works by document. Thus, it was not practical to expand use of the newspaper-oriented system to the business office.

Case #2: Audit Group, Large Manufacturing Firm

This office produces 2,900 lines of typing per day. Unweighted production values indicate a need for 1.5 VDT machines. (Good production levels are assumed.) The question is whether to round up or to round down. Weighted line counts provide the answer.

The workload of this group involves a great deal of statistical typing. Tables and financial schedules are regularly produced. The audit reports go through several levels of reviews. Rarely does a report survive unscathed. Substantial rewrites are common.

Weighted line counts are computed by multiplying the number of lines of typing in each category by the appropriate factors listed in Table 6.2. The computation looks like this:

Actual Lines/Day	Weighting Factor	Weighted Lines
580 statistical lines	2×	1,160
1,160 original lines	1.5×	1,740
1,160 revised lines (20%)	1.2×	1,390
		4,290

Dividing the weighted total of 4,290 by 2,200 lines per day — the maximum excellent value — indicates a need for 1.9 machines. Clearly two VDT workstations are required.

STAFFING DECISIONS

At this point, unless you are a very small office, you face a dilemma. You really want and need word processing. But you don't want to fire all those typists. Moreover, your instinctive reaction is that you need both the machines and the people. This is about where we left our newspaper office. What are the choices?

First, you may have to rethink your original assumption. In difficult economic times, it may be necessary to make do with fewer people. In this case, word processing provides a way to keep up production with a smaller staff.

Second, you may want to realign administrative workload. Secretaries who are no longer occupied typing can relieve managers and other personnel of many routine tasks. Your questionnaires and interviews should help you identify some of these. Edward R. Smith, president of Smith Olewine Consultants, has developed a good model for analyzing categories of administrative support, as follows:

(a) Mechanical — copying, making travel arrangements, ordering supplies
(b) Judgmental — routing mail, answering public inquiries, bookkeeping
(c) Paraprofessional — conducting research, composing reports, standing in at meetings

Most offices tend to burden secretarial jobs with mechanical tasks. There is no question they need to be done. But most secretaries enjoy the other levels of work and are quite capable of handling them. Work with the organization to assign more judgmental and paraprofessional tasks to qualifed secretaries.

The third choice is simply to do more work. Speaking from experience, this is the preferred option. Most offices don't turn to WP unless a problem exists in the first place. There are usually substantial backlogs of one kind or another. The first accomplishment in any new WP system may be that the filing gets done.

The Quick Check Method

Most WP studies end up with some kind of cost justification. For example, the results of a study may indicate a need for five VDT machines. To justify the expense, the company finds it must reduce three clerical positions. This computation then becomes the basis for establishing the new staffing level. To me, the logic of this approach has always seemed faulty. It assumes that the staffing level of the existing operation is correct to begin with, something I am not ready to accept as a given.

A better method for determining staff needs is to start with a good systems design. Use everything you know about the organization. Take into account document samples, line counts, non-typing work, interviews, workload changes, backlogs, the works. From this, design a system that represents the best combination of people, machines and work for your organization.

When you have a design that makes sense, then see if you can justify it. Consider cost or any other tangible or intangible benefit that you have established as a study objective. If the justification doesn't prove out, then make the necessary compromises. But don't assume that numbers of machines and personnel are the only variables. Keep working within the framework of your original objectives until you have a system that works.

Knowing when a design makes sense may not always be obvious. For this, I have devised a simple test. It is based on information developed for other purposes. But it works well just the same.

A number of organizations have done statistical samplings of secretarial workload distribution. The surprising thing is that the breakdown of activities by time conforms to a fairly consistent pattern. Typing usually accounts for about 20% of the workload. The biggest item is time spent away from the desk.

Table 6.3 is based on studies of a large number of organizations. Study A was conducted by the International Information/Word Processing Association; Study B by Truax, Smith and Associates.

Table 6.3 Secretarial Workload Distribution

	Study A	Study B
Away from desk	24.7%	30.0%
Typing	19.7%	19.4%
Clerical	12.8%	19.2%
Communications	13.9%	12.2%
Waiting for work	18.4%	8.9%
Dictation	2.3%	3.3%
Other	8.2%	7.0%

Interruptions average every 11 minutes.

These figures highlight workload distribution problems. They demonstrate how important it is to reduce time away from the desk. In designing WP systems, the figures can also be used another way. As an example, let's consider a specific case.

A Government Office's Experience

A medium-size city government has exceptional backlogs in filing, typing and other secretarial work. A WP study is done. It shows that there are 40 secretarial personnel handling typing and administrative workload. Using electric typewriters, these 40 people produce 10,000 lines of typing per day. This is the full-time equivalent of 16 typists. In other words, 40% of the secretarial resource is dedicated to this task.

With the addition of VDT and other WP equipment, the number of full-time equivalent typists drops from 16 to 8 positions. Only eight people are needed for typing; we can cut the remaining staff from 40 to 32 people. However, given the backlogs, this leads to the same problem we have now: too few people for administrative tasks.

A better alternative is to reduce one or two positions at most. This leaves us with 38 positions, eight of which will be dedicated to typing. In other words, 21% of the secretarial resources will now be spent on this task. A reasonable work force remains for other duties. Based on what Table 6.3 says is typical of most offices, this leaves us with an organization in good balance.

Good balance indicates good design. However, we still must test our design with some kind of cost-benefit justification. We still need to know whether we can afford our ideal situation. We may be forced into compromises. The important point is to begin our formal justification using a design that meets all needs, rather than one designed around word processors and typists alone.

COST-BENEFIT COMPARISON

The Justification Process

A new system is usually justified based on a formal comparison of benefits and costs, plusses and minuses. If the plusses win, the design should be implemented. Otherwise, back to the drawing board. There are two reasons for doing a justification. First, you have to test your plan: Does it make sense? Will it meet your stated objectives? Second, you have to test these answers against the cost of the new system. Is it worth doing?

Once you've convinced yourself and your team, you must convince everybody else. Even if you're in charge, this selling job makes sense. Your staff may not have the right of refusal, but sometimes it's hard to tell the difference. Try to win their cooperation by sharing the results of your analysis.

Most new systems are justified by increasing productivity or reducing costs. Actually, they are two sides of the same coin. The goal is the same: more work, or better work, per employee. Don't lost sight of this as you begin to budget for your new system.

The problem with technology is that it costs money — less and less each year, but still it requires an outlay of cash (or credit). As we just discussed, the most common reaction is to compensate for this outlay with a demonstrated dollar

. . . Can we afford to change?

savings. However, this approach doesn't always fit with what technology does best: increase an office's capacity for work. At the risk of using a cliche, sometimes you have to spend money to make money. The example below illustrates the point:

A two-person law office has a single legal secretary. There is no thought of saving enough in salaries to pay for the WP equipment. The secretary must be there full-time.

The secretary earns $1,200 per month. The partners lease a word processor for $400 a month, one third the secretary's salary. The secretary's productivity using the new equipment goes up 50%. The law firm is ahead of the game. The expense is justified by the ability to produce more work.

Proving Productivity Gains

Unfortunately, productivity gains are hard to prove. Rarely is a real life case as straightforward as this example. And productivity gains, if they occur, can often only be measured after the equipment is in. Catch-22 all over again: the only way to prove you need the system is to get it; and you can't get it until you prove you need it. What to do?

If you did your homework at the beginning of the survey, you took a hard look at your office workload and decided which problems needed solving.

These you formulated into a set of objectives. They became the basis for your study and analysis.

Your objectives might be tangible (measurable): reduce staffing by 10%; reduce turnaround time by four hours; eliminate all backlogs; generate two more contract proposals per month.

Or they might be intangible: improve the appearance of letters; permit extra revisions; eliminate mechanical routine from skilled secretaries' jobs; or, through list processing, allow users expanded access to information in their files.

Some tangible and most intangible benefits relate to productivity gains. By defining your original objectives carefully and by stating them in quantitative terms, it is possible to prove the merit of a system which initially will cost more than it saves. You can, and should, check your findings once WP is in place. Some vendors even make it easy by offering a no-strings trial rental. The cost is usually reasonable and you can eat your cake (the proof) and have it, too (no commitments until the proof is in).

A Return-on-Investment Analysis

Justifications based on intangible benefits are necessarily somewhat subjective. In theory, return-on-investment analyses (or ROIs) are not. This process compares the hard dollar costs of your current operation with those of the proposed operation. At some point, usually about the third year, the change is supposed to pay for itself.

The problem with ROIs is that they always come out. Unless you have a very honest auditor on your team, the temptation is to play with the numbers until they work. The result is often a system that looks good on paper; the right number of machines and people have been traded. Yet the changes rarely take place as planned.

The problem is not necessarily bad systems design. Indeed, with its new WP, the office may be functioning better than ever. The problem is that ROIs tend to be an artificial process. Rarely is there a commitment to the plan itself, once its mission of bringing the equipment in is finished.

ROIs do have their place. When they take intangible benefits into account, and when they are scrupulously objective, ROIs can be an important analytical tool.

The basic components of an ROI are summarized here. There are some additional calculations. These include present value and opportunity cost analyses, among others. They are used to adjust for inflation and other uses for the same dollars. Your own accountant can tell you how these techniques are applied in your organization. However, if you are on the right track, the ROI will probably come out whether you allow for inflation or not.

Making the Calculations

To calculate the true cost of the present system, compute the following:

(a) Salaries for all typing and administrative secretaries, including over time and fringe benefits
(b) Costs for temporary secretarial services or service bureaus
(c) Rental, lease and maintenance costs for existing word processors and typewriters
(d) Media and supplies costs

To calculate the true cost of the proposed system, compute:

(a) Salaries for all WP and AS personnel, including overtime and fringe benefits. Include the cost of any new supervisory or management positions, messengers, proofreaders, etc.
(b) Costs for outside services, if any
(c) Cost of equipment (hardware, software, delivery and installation)
(d) Cost of financing, if any, for lease
(e) Residual cost to you to own equipment after lease has expired
(f) Cost of maintenance
(g) Cost of furniture, drapes, sound deadeners, static free materials, air conditioning
(h) Cost of site preparation
(i) Cost of training

For both the present and the proposed system, calculate the total annual cost for five years. The costs may vary from year to year. For example, if you purchase hardware, all equipment costs will occur in the first year. You may compute your ROI that way, or you may prorate the cost equally over five years.

Either way, calculate the cumulative difference in price between the two systems until you reach the cross-over point. This is the time at which the total cost for the new system is less than that for the old. If you will make it in three years or less, and if your process was objective, you now have a systems justification that no one can quarrel with. You can stretch your cross-over point to five years, the expected useful life of most office systems. However, your accountant may not approve.

At last! Now you can stop thinking about if and start thinking about how. You have your machines and even your staffing fairly well in mind. How do you go about setting it up? How do you arrange everything? The next chapter tells all.

7
Setting Up Shop

If you are the lucky user of one word processor — and no more — you can safely skip most of this chapter. Not that you aren't welcome, of course. But the great debate about whether to centralize or decentralize word processing won't apply to you. You can skip to the sections on personnel, physical planning and daily operations. The rest of you, though, need to start here.

CENTRALIZED WORD PROCESSING

Before going into the pros and cons of centralized WP, let's review a little history. In history, if nothing else, WP definitely follows after DP. It arrived on the scene a good decade later. Over the years, the users and managers of data processing have learned some lessons that WP must face as well.

A Very Short Course on the History of Data Processing

When data processing made its debut in the world of offices and information management, there was no choice but to centralize. The cost of the equipment alone required that. Moreover, operating the equipment required a host of systems analysts and programmers. There was simply no way to provide individual managers or departments with their own computers.

But there were problems with this arrangement. For the purposes of our discussion, we'll group these under four headings: control, priority conflicts, communication and responsiveness.

Control, or Who's in Charge?

Good management theory says that a manager charged with a responsibility needs control over the resources to fulfill that responsibility. Data processing concerns itself with information. No resource is more vital. Yet in a centralized DP environment, each manager must compete for attention with everyone else. Control over this resource lies outside the manager's control.

Priority Conflicts, or Who's First?

The problem is more complex than simple control. When individual users are competing for attention, top management must establish priorities. On a day-to-day basis, this is difficult to coordinate. As a result, priority conflicts are not always resolved in the best manner for the organization as a whole.

Communication, or Why Don't You Understand What I Mean?

In a centralized DP operation, the programmers and analysts serve all the departments in a company. The DP staff are specialists in DP, and generalists in everything else. Users spend a disproportionate amount of time explaining their applications to the DP staff. There is a very valuable — and often underrated — communication established when users and DP staffers speak each other's language. Too often, the need to assign DP staff to a variety of problems interrupts this communication process.

Responsiveness, or What Do You Mean I Have to Wait until Monday?

Even if everything else goes right, it usually takes longer to get results back from a centralized support group. Routine reports may cause no trouble, but special requests bog down. There is more coordination and more arranging when two departments are involved. This means delays.

New Trends in Data Processing

The DP industry has responded to this set of problems with distributed data processing. Individual departments do have control over their computers, usually dedicated minicomputers. These are linked, or networked, together to provide the total information system the organization needs.

This analysis is an oversimplification, of course. First of all, there are still many centralized computer systems. And many do serve quite well. Secondly, there are still problems with the design and networking of distributed data processing systems. But our point here still holds: a definite trend toward decentralization has been established.

Users started the trend. But technology has made it possible. Computers are cheaper than ever before. A department can afford to own a computer. Ten years ago this was an impossibility.

Computers are also far more sophisticated. High-level user languages are pre-programmed into the systems. It's like having a list of all the possible questions stored inside. To request a new kind of report, you simply string the right sequence of questions together — in English. You no longer have to be a programmer to ask a question of a computer.

The Politics of Centralized Word Processing

What does all this have to do with WP? First of all, whether you centralize DP or WP you will likely run into the same set of problems. These same four problems can be critical when something as valuable as WP is at issue.

Control

If DP is information, WP is communications — an equally important resource. It is every manager's link with the rest of the world: top management, employees, customers. No one willingly gives up control over communications.

Priority Conflicts

These are always difficult to manage. Let's look at a specific case. A large engineering organization sets up a WP center. Dictation equipment is installed. Encouraging use of dictation is the center manager's top priority. A policy of processing all dictated work first is established. When the president finds out, he hits the ceiling. The company's priorities are engineering projects. Designers' work comes first, regardless of how it arrives. Yet even within that established priority, there are still difficult conflicts that must be resolved.

Communication Problems

To some extent, these are built into a centralized WP operation. In a regular working relationship, typists learn to handle individual authors differently. Some tolerate editing, others don't. Terminology and handwriting become familiar. More importantly, authors can communicate their needs directly. Filling out forms and following complex procedures to get a letter typed is not necessarily good use of an author's time. In the rush to set up WP centers, the inherent value of author-typist communication has been overlooked. The very nature of the center deliberately restricts author-typist communication. Usually, authors are not allowed contact with anyone except the supervisor.

Responsiveness

It's often a matter of perception. Related problems, such as slow turnaround time, can occur whether typing is centralized or not. However, the frustration is easier to deal with locally. The reasons for delay there are apparent, whereas in a center it is usually cause for feeling ignored.

There are some other, more subtle ways in which centers are unresponsive. For example, centers tend to impose a uniform standard of typing on the entire organization. This inhibits special requests, even though the standard format may not be suitable in all cases.

Some Advantages of Centralized Word Processing

This does not mean that there aren't some very good applications for word processing centers. Properly managed, they have a definite role in office systems. Here are a few examples.

Production Typing

A firm of civil engineers designs and constructs bridges and dams under government contract. The design specifications are long, technical documents. Some canned paragraphs, or boilerplate, are pulled from the diskette library for use in several different specifications. Many authors work on the documents, which also go through multiple levels of review. Different sections may even be at different stages of revision. As deadlines approach, several typists may work on a single section at the same time. This kind of typing is best handled in a WP center.

Special Typing

A university research group of 60 authors also produces technical papers. Only one or two authors are involved in any given project. During the research phase of projects, little typing is required. When reports are typed, however, they often include complex scientific notation. Special printers with extra character sets are required. The sporadic nature of the work and the need for expensive specialized equipment make this a good choice for a WP center.

Centralized Dictation

Many companies use dictation to support field personnel. For example, a salesperson prepares the day's orders for an after-hours report. When the phone rates are low, the orders are called in. In the morning, the center staff transcribes the night's work. The sales orders go out to be filled; the summary report is on the regional manager's desk before 10:00 a.m. Centralized dictation works best when typing is centralized as well.

DECENTRALIZED WORD PROCESSING

For letters, reports, internal communications and the like, authors usually expect quick turnaround time on both originals and revisions. They often need to recall documents even as they are in process. Direct communication with the typist is highly valued. This kind of work does not fare well in centers.

New Technology Makes It Possible

WP technology has changed, too. You can buy a machine today for half the price of seven years ago. It is even possible to use it less than eight hours a day and still be cost-effective. And, like computers, word processors have become easier to use. Typists do not have to memorize as much coding. The machine is programmed to complete an entire procedure, such as reversing paragraphs, at the touch of a single button. With VDTs, training time is shortened from five to two days on many systems. It is even practical to train several typists who will take turns using a single system.

There are several alternatives. Examples provide the best explanation.

Decentralization to the Work Group Level

The headquarters office of a coal mining company has 187 employees. They are housed on five floors of a restored 19th century brick office building. The company has organized its work groups to conform as closely as possible to the natural divisions of floors in the building. In descending order, the floors are assigned to the Executive Offices, Business Development and Marketing, Administration and Personnel, Mining Exploration and Operations, and Finance and Accounting. Primary mining operations are, of course, dispersed to the field.

This company chose to set up WP operations floor by floor. Their job was made easier by the physical separation of component offices. But the same principle can be applied wherever a natural work group boundary exists.

Expenses are kept down by carefully selecting the right machines for each floor. For instance, the fifth floor Executive Office gets by with electronic typewriters. Occasional longer documents are sent to the Finance secretary, on the first floor, who is equipped with a VDT. This secretary is cleared for confidential executive work.

VDTs are also used in Business Development and in Mining Exploration and Operations. Blind machines are adequate for Marketing and for Administration and Personnel. The diskettes used for the blind machine in Marketing are compatible with those of the VDT in Business Development. Both groups are on the same floor. Thus, Marketing also has access to sophisticated editing when needed.

When work groups are harder to define, the work measurement study can help. Tabulate the results by author rather than by secretary. Look for authors whose work requires similar equipment, and who are reasonably close to each other. Don't worry too much about organizational labels at this stage. If users balk at sharing a system between two offices, remind them that the alternative is probably a center remote from both of them.

Decentralization with or without Specialization

In a center, the staff is highly specialized; there are supervisors, operators, editors, proofreaders and messengers. Some tasks may overlap, but all tasks are directly associated with typing. Administrative tasks are generally handled outside the center by AS specialists. These people, in turn, may be centralized or not.

In a decentralized situation, the typists may specialize or not. It depends upon the volume of typing, the length and complexity of documents and the preference of the organization. Let's go back to our mining company for a minute.

In the Executive Office, the secretaries do not specialize. Principals and secretaries are still closely identified with each other. While not a complete return to the one-on-one relationship, it would be safe to say that this floor is rather traditional.

Neither is there WP/AS specialization in Business Development and Marketing on the fourth floor. The secretaries in these groups traded off. Some days, one would do all the typing — the next day it would be someone else.

This arrangement offers several advantages. In the course of a day, the secretary who does the typing is not subjected to frequent interruptions. As the level of concentration improves, so does the quality of the work. In interviews, incidentally, secretaries most often cite interruptions as their worst problem.

Because the secretaries rotate duties, each job has a reasonable amount of variety. Each secretary is able to maintain a good skill level on the equipment. Having backup personnel available is never a problem. Again, during interviews, more than 80% of the secretaries I talk to list variety as what they like best about their jobs. Rotating WP/AS specialization is one means of having the best of both worlds.

On the second floor, where technical typing relating to mining operations was done, the secretaries chose permanent specialization. The AS secretaries were trained as back-up WP typists, but rarely used the equipment. The secretaries were free to choose their specializations when the equipment was installed. The entire support staff was viewed as a work unit with parallel pay structures.

Complete Decentralization

It is, of course, possible to decentralize completely. The hospital we talked about in the early chapters did just that. Separate systems are installed in Administration, Finance, Medical Staff Support and Nursing Administration. Each office has enough work to justify its own machine. Each has different requirements. And each is physically separated from the others.

Other Alternatives

In very large organizations, a hybrid arrangement is possible. A large insurance firm processes every kind of document from repetitive letters to contracts to technical underwriting reports. A large shared-resource multi-station system is installed in the basement. This center handles the big jobs, plus overflow from the smaller systems distributed throughout the company. These stand-alone units are located in specific organizations where the daily volume justifies dedicated equipment.

Another company has devised an innovative use of a shared-resource system.

The main unit — three workstations and two printers — is in a center. Other workstations and printers are distributed to strategic locations in the building. They are not assigned to specific departments. Secretaries may reserve time at these workstations in blocks of two hours or less. Anything longer requires management approval.

On the face of it, this sounds like a system guaranteed to fail. It causes secretaries to be away from their desks. It is difficult to budget time requirements accurately. But it works. Good management and a cooperative attitude among the secretaries make the difference.

DICTATION SYSTEMS

This is a good time to talk about dictation. Certainly, if you plan to centralize WP, you may want to consider dictation as one way of getting work to your center. Also, if you have a large proportion of short documents — usually two pages or less — dictation can be used effectively.

This section could almost be subtitled: "If it's so good, how come no one wants to use it?" The fact is, dictation really is a very good idea. Equally true, according to industry estimates, is that two-thirds of the machines installed are not used. What accounts for the discrepancy?

First of all, if you want to originate a letter, you have three choices: longhand, shorthand, or machine dictation. You can write at about 15 words per minute (wpm) while you can speak at about 60 to 80 wpm. Thus, you can dictate the average 150-word business letter in 2.5 minutes, 25% of the time it would take to write it.

Secondly, transcription is also easier for a typist to work with. Shorthand is transcribed 30% faster than longhand. Machine dictation is even faster.

As you can see, dictation is faster not just for the author but for the typist as well. Shorthand dictation has the obvious defect that it ties up two people during the dictation phase. Machine dictation is the clear winner in a head to head contest over productivity. According to Datapro Research Corporation, you can save as much as $1.40 on the average business letter by using dictation machines.

Why Dictation Is Underutilized

Why, then, is it so underutilized? There are several reasons. Most authors are comfortable with longhand. The organization, or more particularly the WP study team, may perceive a productivity problem. The authors do not. The timing of the change to dictation is usually arbitrary. It coincides with the study team's new awareness of a problem that has always existed. The very fact that the change is arbitrary sets some authors against it and makes it difficult to motivate others.

Another problem is that most organizations strive for total conversion. They do not recognize that different kinds of work are simpler to adapt to dictation than others. Reactive dictation — a response to a letter or completing the items of a form — is always easier to learn than creative dictation. If you do plan a major conversion, work with authors to identify good applications.

One of the worst ways to implement central dictation is to blackmail authors into using it. The typical approach is to process dictated work on a priority basis, letting handwritten work take second place on the WP center's schedule. Needless to say, authors who are not comfortable with dictation resent this treatment. And, as we discussed earlier, this often results in mismanagement of work priorities. A handwritten project report may be far more important than a dictated memo-to-the-file on a routine staff meeting. Arbitrary priority scheduling defeats the purpose of the WP system.

The market is competitive. There are many excellent machines. Unlike word processors, dictation equipment prices usually equate with performance. For that reason, this book will not dedicate a great deal of space to equipment selection, other than to introduce you to the marketplace.

Types of Equipment

There are four principal kinds of dictation systems: endless loop, distributable media, desk top and portable. Most vendors who make one make all four. Their relative merits are as follows:

Endless loop — holds 180 minutes of dictation (more or less) on a continuous band of tape, which never runs out. Transcription can begin before dictation is complete. Thus, it is very attractive to hospitals. When the band is full, work can be distributed to one or two transcriptionists only. Thus, endless loop is unattractive for large accumulations of dictation. The unit cost is high, but is economical for supporting many authors in a centralized system. (See Figure 7.1.)

Distributable media — uses a series of cassettes (many sizes) or disks, each

72   THE WORD PROCESSING HANDBOOK

Figure 7.1   Endless Loop Dictation System

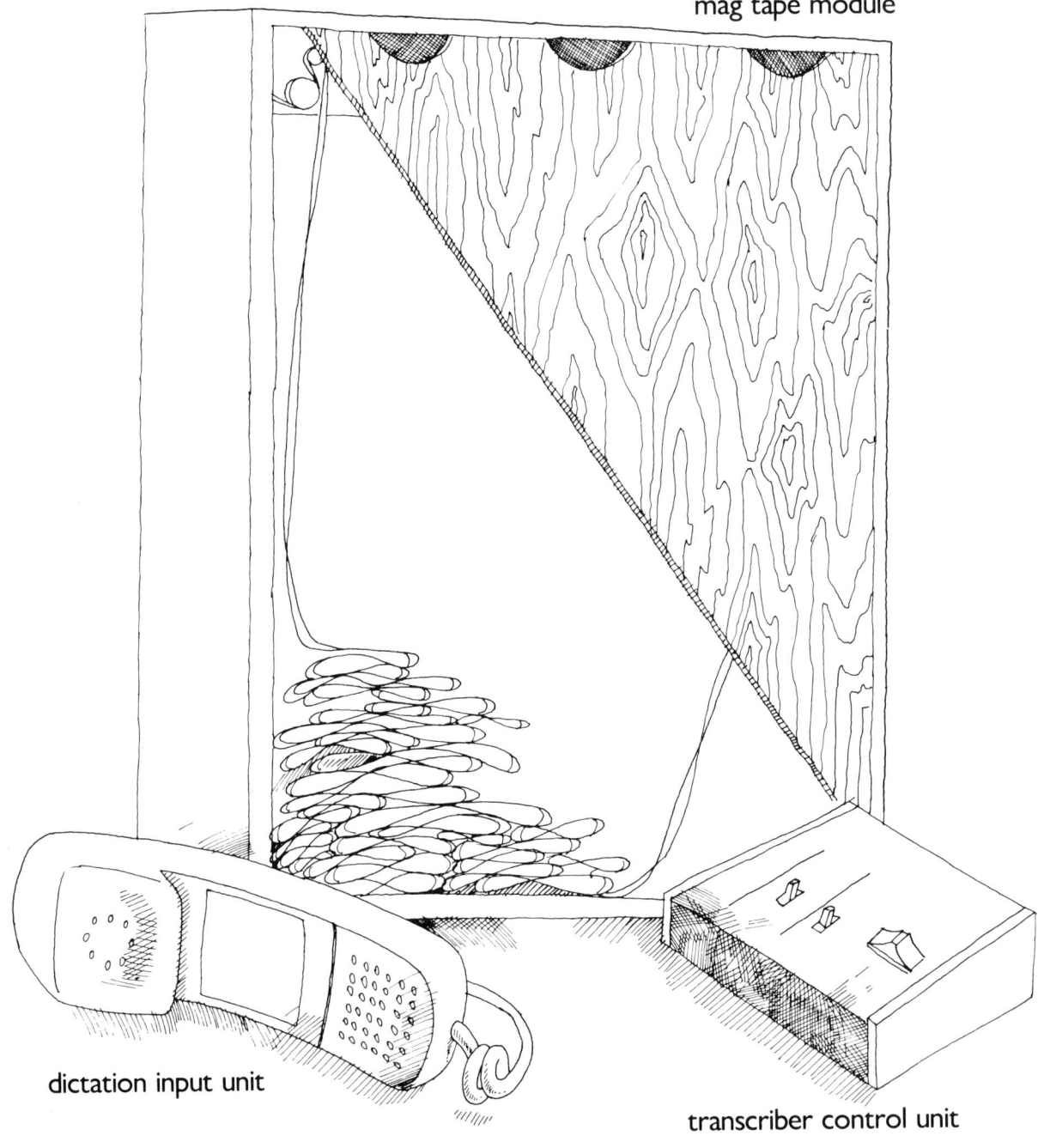

capturing 6 to 30 minutes dictation. Cassettes and the like are good for workload distribution. One machine usually holds six hours total. The unit cost is even higher than endless loop. (See Figure 7.2.)

Desk top — is much more expensive per author than either of the centralized systems described above. Some machines double as transcribers and dictating systems. Usually, you need one of each. (See again Figure 7.2.)

Portable — systems with full features are too bulky for most users. Thin models are attractive, but sacrifice indexing capabilities. Look for separate microphone and speaker for better sound. Conference microphone adaptors allow pickup of distant speakers. Hand motions should be natural.

Features

Special features worth noting include the following:

Indexing — offers the ability to cue transcriptionist directly to an instruction with a special electronic signal.

Monitors — are used in central dictation systems. Very sophisticated (and expensive) monitors indicate all work waiting, work done, priorities, author statistics and typing statistics. Others simply show work waiting to be transcribed. For user charge-back systems, workload monitors are useful.

Variable speed control (VSC) — allows the transcriptionist to vary speed without distorting sound. Very useful for authors who speak too slowly.

Input Options

For centralized systems, there are several input options. Their relative merits are as follows:

A touch-tone phone — allows anyone to input. They offer a full range of functions: back-up, fast forward, etc. Telephone interface equipment is required.

A dial phone — allows anyone to input, but with limited control. The author cannot go back or forward easily. Interface is again required. Touch-tone adaptors are available.

The hard-wired option — is a hand-held telephone-like unit wired to the

Figure 7.2 Distributable Media Dictation Equipment

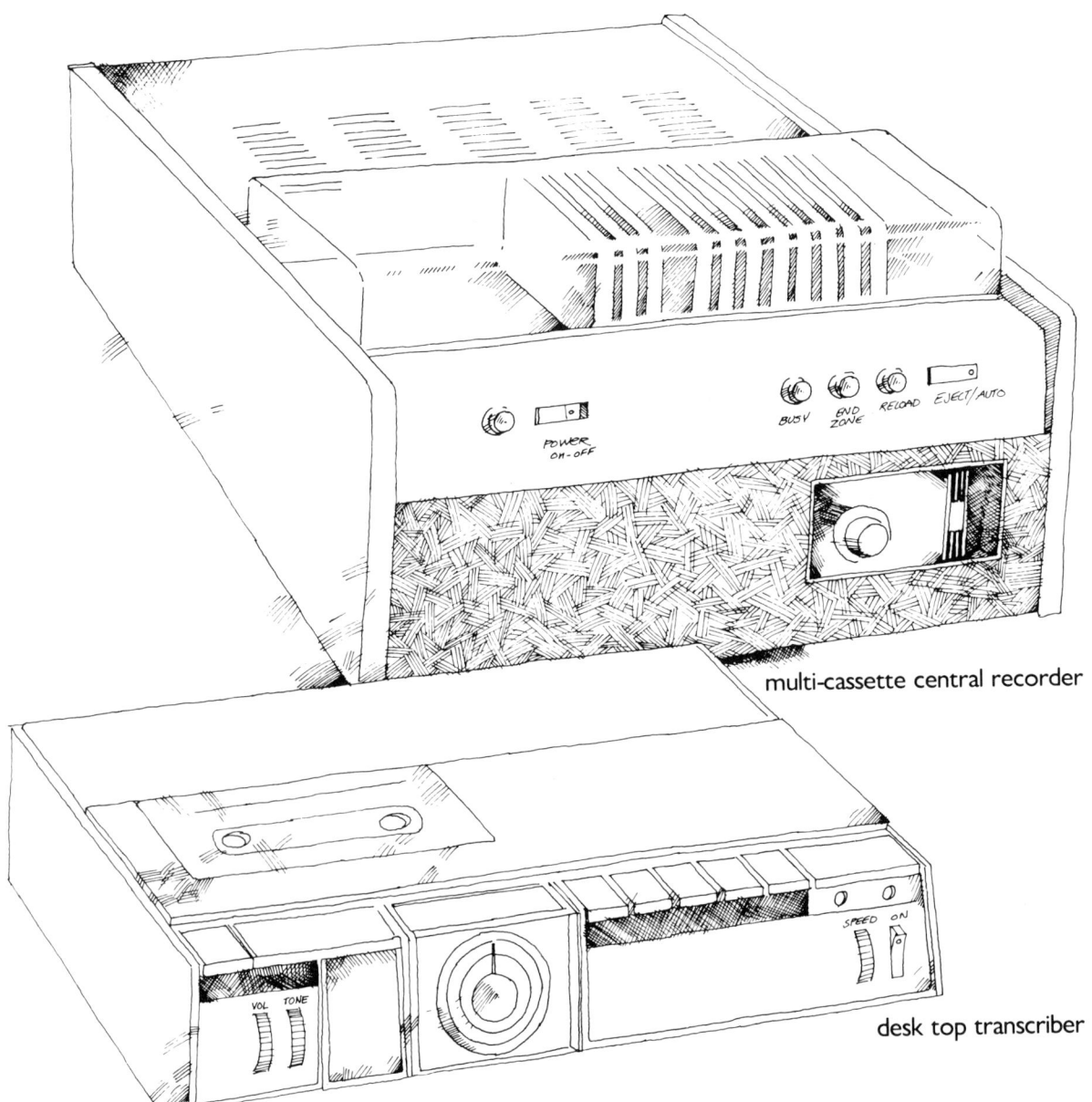

center. It is relatively cheap until moved. Wiring costs are high. The special unit frees authors' phones for normal use.

Peripheral Issues

In the U.S., since the Carterfone decision, you can buy the telephone interface equipment from the vendor. In Canada, you will most likely buy it from the telephone supplier: Trans Canada Telephone System (TCTS) or Canadian National/Canadian Pacific (CN/CP). Telephone lines and interface equipment can add significantly to monthly operating costs. Include them in your cost projections.

No matter how much media is available on a central unit — whether endless loop or distributable media — only one author can have access to the unit at a time. If another author wants to dictate, a second unit is required. Vendors call this the collision factor. Be wary of buying too many back-up units. Unless dictation is well-established — usually in hospitals and law firms — collisions are rarely a problem. Remember all those installed units that are sitting idle.

One last problem with telephone input: interruptions. You start a letter and someone walks in. You can't keep the center unit on hold for a half an hour, so you scrub your effort and start over again later. Maybe this problem is better called frustration. For users who are subject to interruptions, and for users who put constant demands on equipment, desk top rather than central equipment is best.

In addition to traditional dictation systems, a new technology called voice store and forward is now being offered. Its primary emphasis is on streamlining telephone communications, and it is discussed more fully in chapter 13, which deals with electronic mail. However, voice store and forward systems can also streamline the distribution of short intra-office communications to a large number of recipients.

Transcription of the dictated message, typing, proofreading, copying and physical distribution are all eliminated. Instead, the author records a message once. The voice signal is stored on computer media for later access by as many recipients as are designated. Equipment in the recipients' offices alerts them to the waiting message, which they listen to by phone. Although it is too early to predict how people will react to this technology, it is likely to have a major impact on the use of traditional dictation equipment for intra-office communications.

MANAGEMENT OF WP

How should WP be managed? As with everything else, it depends. It's easier to describe what good management does than what it is. First, the WP manager ensures good workload distribution. This means that all WP typists are producing the right amount at the right level of complexity and accuracy. If specific typists do not type full-time, the manager may choose to monitor the rate of equipment utilization instead. Either way, the manager establishes reasonable standards and sees that they are met.

The WP manager is the focal point in the company for all questions and complaints. This person is charged with keeping up-to-date on equipment and recognizing when changes are necessary. This person also is responsible for resolving priority conflicts before they become major conflicts.

One of the most important aspects of the manager's job is the redistribution of work among offices. During peak periods in one group, there may be more work than the typists can handle. At the same time, another group may be slow. In decentralized operations, it is essential that the WP manager have the authority to redistribute work when this occurs.

There are three ways to sell this concept in an organization. If you're the president, you can order it. Or, you can threaten users that unless they comply, all typing will be pulled into a WP center. Some minor tampering with work assignments is usually preferable. The third way is to go back to the work measurement. Look at how many typists did work for other groups during the survey. In almost every organization where peaks occur, there is a natural tendency among the typists to redistribute the work themselves. The best response to balky users is to show that the new system represents very little change at all.

Who Should the Manager Be?

If you want to stir up an office, ask this simple question: "Should WP be under DP?" Once that debate is rolling, you can introduce some other possible organizational homes: administrative management, records management, direct reporting to the vice-president. No doubt you will have encouraged a battle that will rage for days.

This book doesn't have any easy answers. From personal experience, good management appears to be as much a function of personality and credibility as it is of organizational location. Thus, the necessary qualifications are listed here, but not necessarily where to find them.

Good Interpersonal Skills

This means understanding people. Supervision and motivation are important. Establishing credibility with managers, authors and secretaries is essential to obtaining their cooperation. A good WP manager will be as effective in dealing with management as in dealing with customers and typists.

Training and Development Skills

Equipment changes mean changes in work habits. The WP manager is charged with bringing about the right kind of changes. Authors must be educated as to what the equipment can do for them. Secretaries and typists must understand how changes in equipment change their role in the office. Knowledge of office methods and procedures is required.

WP Expertise

The manager must be familiar with WP equipment and how to analyze the company's needs. This includes knowing when to call in an expert for special advice.

Printing and Graphics

If the typing function will be expanded to include typography, the WP manager must have some background in photocomposition and graphics. If the WP manager is to be in charge of these functions, of course, advanced professional skills will be necessary.

Is WP Typing Really a Special Skill?

This is a good time to address a very knotty question: are WP typists a special breed — deserving special pay — or not? Before answering this question, it is important to understand that it has two sides.

The management side goes like this: "I invested a lot of money in some new and expensive equipment. It's designed to eliminate the drudgery from a typist's job and make it that much easier. Not only that, my typist was trained to operate this equipment on the job at full pay. And now, I'm being asked for a raise to boot. No way!"

The secretary's side goes like this: "I'm more productive than before. I have a new skill — one that's in demand. If I don't get my raise here, someone else will be glad to pay that salary for a trained WP operator. Bye-bye!"

Both parties are probably right. A WP typist may be no better or more skilled than any other typist. But a trained WP specialist commands a higher salary on the open market. To keep valuable employees, you will probably have to pay them more.

If you are selecting staff to train, there are no rules as to who will be a good candidate. I once worked with two older secretaries who had been on their jobs 28 and 25 years respectively. This, I thought, is a prescription for disaster. However, they were both extremely competent professionals able to appreciate the value of WP immediately. Contrary to my expectations, they excelled at using the machines.

In general, secretaries who have good professional and language skills and who express interest in the equipment will do fine. Allowing people some say in their assignments always helps.

WP Position Descriptions

No two organizations approach position descriptions and pay scales in the same way. For this reason, there is no standard job description for a WP typist. Some offices have several levels of classification. Others need only one.

There is some common ground. The standards for any one item may vary, but each of the following should be addressed in a well-conceived job description, or graduated series of job descriptions, for a WP typist:

(a) Tasks to be performed — transcription of dictated material, editing, proofreading, document assembly and composing documents from general instructions or notes.

(b) Responsibilities — production levels, accuracy standards, supervision given or received, training given or received (management has some responsibilities, too), and coordination with users, management and clients.

(c) Applications — types of work, types of functions (math or list processing), and complexity.

The above list does not include any administrative duties. These must also be addressed. The same types of categories work well: tasks, levels of responsibility and major functions to be supported. Try to break the tasks into three levels: mechanical, judgmental and paraprofessional. This makes it easier to address pay scales somewhat rationally.

Decide whether you want your secretarial support to be task-oriented, principal-oriented, or group-oriented. The former implies some specialization; the latter two represent the more traditional approach. Do not cast off the traditional approach too quickly. It provides more variety and thus more expression of creativity.

FACILITIES

Whether you set up a large shared-resource system in its own room or you put your new word processor in the middle of your desk, there are some important items to plan for.

Space Layout

You will need a minimum of 100 square feet per workstation; more if there are extra-large printers or other special equipment. VDTs should face away from windows and other direct light sources.

Noise

Impact printers, which most word processors use, are noisy. Consider the rating of 66 to 70 decibels for most daisy wheel printers in relation to the following chart:

50 DB (decibels)	can fall asleep
60-64 DB	the ideal range in an office
68 DB	maximum level without discomfort
70 DB	sustained level can damage hearing
79 DB	operator's accuracy begins to drop off
82 DB	some telegraphic printers fit in here

An acoustical hood which fits over the printer will reduce the noise level by three or four DB. Remember that DB reductions are logarithmic; 80 DB is halved at 74 DB, not at 40. Thus, a reduction of three DB is significant.

If you chose an acoustical hood, there are some points to consider in evaluating different manufacturers. How well does the hood handle glare and reflections? How easy is it to insert and remove paper when the hood is on? Will it work with a continuous paper feed (called a forms tractor) or with other sheet feeds? (Most don't.) Does it offer adequate machine ventilation? Your WP equipment vendor can give you a list of manufacturers and help you pick the best one for your machine.

The word processors themselves also make noise. They beep, blow (their cooling fans do, anyway) and in general make their presence known. Acoustical tiles, panels and drapes can be very helpful in eliminating this distraction.

Static Electricity

When static electricity is discharged, a current is set up. This can have a remarkable effect on word processors: it alters their memory circuits. Perfectly good text may suddenly come out garbled. According to James A. Tolzmann, 3M Company's lab manager for static control, a discharge level of 1,000 volts or less is enough to have this effect. Yet most people cannot even feel a discharge level below 3,500 volts.

If you live in a climate where static electricity is a problem, you should take some protective measures. There are antistatic sprays, for example, which usually must be renewed weekly. If you use these sprays, be sure to do so when the machines are turned off. Otherwise the fans suck the spray in, literally gumming up the works.

Antistatic carpets are another possibility. These are also sold as mats, if you do not want to carpet the entire area. These fabrics are woven with special conductive fibers. When you step on the mat or carpet, all static electricity is discharged. The carpets or mats are arranged so that this occurs before you come in contact with the machine.

Dedicated Lines

A dedicated line means an electrical line that runs directly from the machine to the circuit box. There is nothing else on this line: no other word processors, no copy machines and *no* coffee pots. Surges on the line, which occur when these other machines go on and off, have the same effect as static electricity.

Some vendors claim a dedicated line is not necessary. Be skeptical. Especially if you start having unexplained data problems.

As an alternative to a dedicated line, you can also use a power filter. This is a device which plugs into the wall outlet at one end, and into which you plug your word processor at the other. Imbedded in this small but useful gadget are electronics that prevent power surges from reaching your system's delicate microcomputer.

Power filters are often cheaper than dedicated lines, and have the advantage of being portable should you decide to move your system. If you plan to use one, be sure to check with your vendor first. It is important that the vendor accept the filter as adequate protection for your machine. Otherwise, in the event of damage to your microcomputer, you might find that your maintenance contract does not cover you.

Screen Problems

The biggest problem is glare. There are overlays which can reduce glare. Vendors usually offer these. Eye strain is also a problem. Some screens permit reversing of the character and background colors. Others display characters double-size as an operator option. Still others permit tilting of the screen at different angles. All of these features are helpful.

Many people question whether there are health hazards associated with sitting in front of a screen all day. At present, no definitive answer has been given. However, government studies indicate the hazards are not expected to be significant. Boredom and restricted movement rather than radiation seem to be the problem.

SUPPLIES AND MEDIA

Diskettes

With certain exceptions, you do not have to buy your diskettes for storage (or, for that matter, ribbons or printwheels) from your equipment vendor. Standard commercial sources are usually much cheaper. However, it is wise to get your vendor's approval before using other brands. (See chapter 9 for a description of diskettes.)

Diskette Head Cleaners

The technology of recording on a diskette is not very different from that of recording on your cassette tape deck at home. If you take good care of your cassette deck, you periodically clean the recording heads to remove dust and loose iron oxide particles. (Magnetic media are coated with iron oxide, which sometimes flakes a little.)

Your word processor needs cleaning too, but it hasn't been possible to do it yourself. Now there are commercial diskette head cleaners available. They look like a diskette and are loaded the same way. This little bit of maintenance makes sense, but many head cleaners are too abrasive. Check with your vendor before using one.

Diskette Filing

There are any number of special products on the market. These include special binders with pockets; file folders with pockets; and even desk top or wall-hanging file arrangers. Any of these is adequate, as long as two functions are served: retrieval and protection.

Retrieval means being able to find something on a diskette regardless of when it was typed or who typed it. If several revisions exist, it also means finding the correct one. To some extent, the word processors themselves aid this function by providing automatic indexes and document histories. Some systems permit development of a master index covering all diskettes or an entire disk file in a single place.

All the machine can tell you, however, is what diskette or disk to look for. Finding it in the files is another task. File procedures for media must be established and carefully maintained.

There are several possibilities for arranging material on diskettes: by subject, chronological, by typist, or by author (or work group).

The latter method generally works best. Subject filing is too complex in a multi-author environment. Straight chronological filing packs diskettes more efficiently, but there is no logic to fall back on when the index is silent. Filing by typist gets confusing, especially when someone leaves. Author filing does give you something to fall back on. If the index doesn't help, at least you know which diskette to start looking on when the author wants a third draft.

Protecting media means two things: securing the information and securing the diskettes or disks themselves. In a diskette system, your best information security is to lock confidential diskettes away. Erase them as soon as possible. Disk security usually involves a series of operator and document passwords. (See chapter 9.) Each of these methods is acceptable.

In addition, all diskettes must be secured from office hazards: flying coffee, creeping cigarette ash and floating dust. Humidity is also a problem. If you plan to store material on a diskette for more than six to eight months, it is wise to copy the material to a fresh diskette at least that often. Otherwise, there is a risk of deterioration.

For storage media of exceptional value, off-site duplication is recommended. For example, a set of master paragraphs for specifications might involve many long hours of keyboarding. The text is a long-term value to the company. It takes only minutes to copy the diskette or disk and store it somewhere safe from an office disaster.

Ribbons

Many businesses use recycled ribbons for their machines. In point of fact, this is a misnomer. The ribbons are new; it's the cartridges that are reused. You save yours and exchange them with the supplier. (Not usually your equipment vendor.) You can save up to 40% on ribbon costs in this way.

Print Wheels

Metal print wheels give a marginally sharper image than plastic ones. Unless you are doing multi-part forms, however, it probably doesn't matter. Plastic is usually cheaper.

Paper Feeds

There are three common types of paper feeds: continuous forms tractors, single sheet feeds and dual sheet feeds. Envelope feeds are also available. The first requires perforated paper. The sprockets in the tractor link up with the holes in the paper. In high-speed line printers, this is the only way to keep the paper straight.

Sheet feeds, of course, are nicer. You don't have to use special paper. You avoid all the problems of spot gluing your letterhead or having torn computer paper edges. But sheet feeds are not as reliable. They have the same problems you do when you insert a piece of paper into the machine: it doesn't always go in straight. As a general rule, single sheet feeds are more reliable than doubles. However, this technology is improving rapidly, and reliable dual sheet/envelope feeds are being introduced.

HOW TO EVALUATE ON-GOING OPERATIONS

There are two questions to be answered when evaluating WP operations: how well is an individual typist doing and how well is the service itself delivered?

Individual Performance Evaluation

This method is necessary, of course, as part of any good personnel management program. Measuring production levels and accuracy can be a valid component of this process. Self-measuring evaluation systems based on quantifiable goals are very useful. They provide the employee with an objective way to assess progress; they avoid the subjective assessment of favorites and personalities.

Services Evaluation

Assessing employee performance is not the same thing as measuring how well the system is meeting the company's needs. Again, there are two ways to get at this.

Many companies continually monitor production. If a work measurement study was done initially, actual production is compared to projected requirements. When the new system starts to back up, it is easy to check whether the volume has increased faster than expectations. Typically, usage is 20% over projections.

Unless you are planning to charge user departments for services, however, daily monitoring of individual production is expensive. Line counts are difficult to compute. To be fair, they should be weighted. Revision lines in particular are difficult to deal with. Spot measurement at randomly selected periods may prove just as effective.

Many centers that do measure output simplify matters by using a page overlay. By preparing a single-spaced and double-spaced overlay, it is easy to tally the page total quickly. Most overlays are set up for 10-pitch, which means 10 characters per inch. If your document is 12-pitch, multiply the line count on the overlay by 1.33 to account for the extra keystrokes. If your document is proportionally typed, which makes even more efficient use of a page, multiply your 10-pitch line count by 1.37 to obtain an accurate charge.

Another way to simplify productivity measuring is to count pages rather than lines. The line counts can then be estimated, as shown in Table 7.1.

The character counts are included to help you understand the relationship between pages of text and storage. The vendors use 2,000 characters per page, which is a reasonable average. However, when they claim an electronic typewriter with 8,000 characters of storage will hold four pages, that is stretching things a bit.

One way to understand storage is to relate it to a 30-inch file drawer. There

Table 7.1 Line/Page Relationships

Average word	=	5 characters plus space
Average line	=	65-70 characters (12 words)
Average page	=	30 lines (2,000 characters)
Single-spaced letter	=	60 lines (4,200 characters)
Double-spaced letter	=	30 lines (2,000 characters)
Single-spaced legal-size	=	72 lines (5,040 characters)
Double-spaced legal-size	=	36 lines (2,520 characters)

are 350 pages of about 2,000 characters each per inch — or 21 million characters in a single drawer.

You should also note that the full-page line counts are divisible by four. This makes it easy to estimate line counts to the nearest quarter page.

An even simpler solution to monitoring WP operations is to look for certain warning signs that the system is in trouble. When these occur, closer attention is needed.

- *Slow turnaround time:* Four hours is a good standard for letters and short documents. Longer means trouble. Chronic complaints from users should not be allowed to develop.

- *Users by-pass:* Any time users are going out of their way to avoid using your WP system, you have a problem.

- *Priority management problems:* If chronic, these must be addressed.

- *Low morale/high turnover:* Low pay may be the answer, or it may be a feeling of too many restrictions and too much isolation in the center. Great care should be taken to resolve this situation.

- *Poor control; retrieval problems:* This means WP staff cannot find previously recorded material when it is called for a second time. Or they use the wrong version of a frequently revised document.

- *Excessive paperwork:* Watch the amount of time that authors, supervisors and typists spend filling out forms to get work to and from the WP machine. Don't set up too many communications barriers. And don't institutionalize a permanent WP study.

8

The Art of Acquiring Word Processors

There is more to the equipment selection process than just pointing your finger at the right machine. There's an art to setting up the selection process so that you really do find the right machine (or machines) for the job.

Unfortunately, as of this writing, the perfect word processor has not been invented. No machine offers everything. On the plus side, of course, the "compleat WP user" is rare. Most offices need some capabilities more than others.

The object of the evaluation process is to devise a set of evaluation criteria and match them with specific vendors' machines. Essentially, you are writing a specification for how you want your equipment to perform. The next chapter tells you how to put a specification together.

Once you have designed your specification, there are a couple of ways to go about selecting the best equipment. Either you can go to the vendors, or they can come to you. The first method means attending a host of demonstrations. The second involves submitting a request for proposals; the vendors respond in writing to your specification. Thereafter, you may want to attend demonstrations of the one or two machines you are most interested in. Each method has its place.

DEMONSTRATIONS

Equipment demonstrations are an essential tool in evaluating WP equipment. Many systems use very different routes to the same end. For instance, on some systems pages are automatically readjusted and renumbered after editing. Other machines require the typist to scan each page and change the breaks if necessary. Yet each machine will claim to offer automatic repagination — as this feature is called — as a capability. It is not enough to know that a machine offers a particular feature you are interested in. You also need to know how easy it is to use.

The demonstrations prepared by the vendors naturally highlight good features. If you attend 10 demonstrations arranged by vendors, you will know the best points about 10 machines. You will not, however, have enough standard information about each machine to do a meaningful comparison. Hence, the specification.

Once you have developed a specification, ask each vendor to respond to it point-by-point during the demonstration. Pay particular attention to the simplicity of operations. If the procedures used to set up an operation don't make sense, ask to see them again.

If you plan to do equations on your word processor, bring a tough sample to the demonstration. Ask to see it run from keyboarding to print. Don't submit the material in advance unless it is exceptionally long. Otherwise, you won't know how hard it was to set up.

At the end of this process, you will have a consistent set of answers about each machine. No longer must you puzzle about a list of strong points which varies from machine to machine, trying to figure out which list makes the most sense. You can now decide which machine does the best job of meeting *your* specification.

WRITTEN PROPOSALS

Your specification will be the same regardless of which method you choose to do your market research. The difference between methods is in the distribution of work. Attending 10 demonstrations is a lot of work for you. Asking 10 vendors to respond in writing is a lot of work for them.

Why do a written request for proposals? There are three principal reasons. First, if you are not sure of the market you can use written bids to narrow the field. It is one way to eliminate extraneous systems from your demonstration schedule. If you do that, though, be fair. Limit your preliminary inquiry to a few key points. For instance, if advanced statistical typing is a prime requirement, cull a list of vendors who are strong in that field. Ask only this short list of vendors to respond to your detailed request for information.

Likewise, if you are looking for a single system for a simple application, written proposals are unnecessary. A telephone survey can help you develop a short list of machines. Demonstrations can tell you the rest.

The second reason for requesting written proposals is to research a complex specification. For example, you may require advanced list processing. You know the machine does sorting and selecting. But you want to know how well it will perform when your entire file is on the system. Obviously, it is not practical to demonstrate this kind of information. The vendor may have to research actual performance limitations. This kind of information is best handled in writing.

The third reason for a formal bid process is to ensure objectivity. This is primarily a concern of public agencies. They must guarantee that each vendor is bidding on exactly the same specification. They must also ensure that the lowest bidder is in an acceptable performance range. Written bids subjected to a predetermined rating process are the best way to satisfy this requirement.

If, for whatever reason, you do choose a formal bid process as your method of selecting equipment, there are some useful tricks of the trade. No doubt, your organization has its own standard language to use for this purpose. But you might want to consider some of these adaptations.

Format

Prepare a two-part specification. List mandatory requirements in one part and lower priorities in the other. Limit your mandatory list to those features you must have. For example, you might include list processing, compatability with your phototypesetter, or the ability to share a printer among three VDT workstations. Use the mandatory list to eliminate the machines that won't work for you. The lower priority or desirable requirements are important, but allow some compromise. They recognize that there is no ideal machine. Draw up a list of the capabilities that have a value to you. You might include automatic repagination, display of proportional spacing, or availability of a 10-key pad on this list. Follow the format outlined in the next chapter, being as selective as possible. Assign a numeric value to each item, say from 5 to 15, depending upon its importance to your operation.

Solicitation

First, develop a list of qualified bidders who can meet your mandatory requirements. The earlier you eliminate the rest the better. You save your time and theirs. Ask those vendors who do qualify to respond to the desirable requirements in your specification, answering each item.

You may split the solicitation process. For example, you may work mandatory requirements first. If the qualified list is short, you may choose to have the vendors complete their responses in an actual demonstration (to your specification). Or, you may complete the entire process with written responses, only viewing the top one or two machines.

Rating Bids

You rate bids to find out which offer the best value for your money. Obviously, low price doesn't tell all. To some extent, you get what you pay for. But not always. In word processing systems, cost is going down. There is usually a price range at which comparable machines, say those with VDTs, are offered. But sometimes an innovator in the market challenges competitors by providing the same capabilities for two or three thousand dollars *less*.

The rating process allows you to compare costs and performance. The first step is to compute each vendor's total points, as established by their answers to items in your specification. For example, you may have allocated 10 points to automatic repagination. One machine does it at the touch of a command key: 10 points. Another is semi-automatic; after repagination, the typist must check each page break: five points. And so on. If you are very concerned about objectivity, have two or three people rate each system, resolving all point discrepancies.

Using the total points, compute a price-performance factor for each word processor. For example, let's say you are looking for a system with three workstations and two printers. You have three qualified bidders. The points for these word processors are 695, 735 and 785 points respectively. Prices range from $58,000 to $61,000 to $67,000 in the same order.

To find the performance-cost ratio, divide the total points by the total price: 695 points divided by $58,000 = .0119; 735 by $61,000 = .0120; and 785 by $67,000 = .0117. In other words, how many points does each dollar buy? In this case, system B proves the best choice. (Don't let the decimal places throw you off. The relative positions of the machines are important, not the absolute value of the numbers.)

Other Ideas

If you're planning a large system, specify the number of workstations but not the configuration. Some vendors may offer a better deal with stand-alone units; others with a shared-resource system. You want to see the best offering, regardless of how it's set up. Surprisingly, because of new offerings, shared-resource systems are not always cheaper — even when eight or more typists are involved.

Discourage flashy bids. You want information, not color brochures. Ask for printed examples of document indexes and document histories. Request unit prices and extended prices (the vendor's projected cost for your total configuration). If the two don't jibe, make sure the vendor's bid includes everything it's supposed to.

If you are acquiring a very large system, or if you are working with a vendor new to the market, request a performance bond. Require that this bond be held until the system has been accepted as performing to specification. Usually, this is 90 to 120 days after installation and training. The bond should cover your total investment up to time of acceptance (rental/lease payments or purchase price).

Ask for references, especially references in your local service area. Call these references. Be very wary of uniformly bad reports. A machine is only as good as its service record.

TO BUY OR NOT TO BUY

The relative cost of a machine changes depending upon how you pay for it. Machine A may be cheap to buy, but expensive to lease. Machine B offers the reverse situation.

Why the difference? It is largely a matter of strategy. Some vendors cannot afford to carry leases or rentals. Their pricing favors purchase. Some finance leases in-house; others use third party (commercial) financing. This affects the rate they can offer prospective customers. You also can make your own financing arrangements.

In comparing the costs for various word processors, make sure you take the acquisition method into account. Don't compare purchase prices if you plan to lease for 36 months. Compare 36-month lease prices instead.

How do these pricing plans work? Purchase is purchase. You own it. You pay freight, installation and maintenance. Rental is rental. You own nothing. The vendor pays all extra costs such as maintenance, because the vendor still owns the machine.

Lease, however, is not always lease. It is usually installment purchase. You pay for the machine; you pay interest; you pay freight, installation and maintenance. And at the end of the lease you may still have to pay 10% or so of the original purchase price to own the equipment.

A government agency can usually cancel a lease early without penalty. They do this by claiming that funds are no longer available. But for everyone else, a lease is as much of a commitment as purchase.

Many people choose leasing because they believe it preserves their freedom to change. They view it as a hedge against obsolescence. If the equipment is outmoded, the rationale goes, we'll get something else. There are two things wrong with this logic. One, you can't do it, or at least not without a substantial penalty. And two, you won't want to.

Most word processors have a useful life of at least three years. The cost of analyzing your needs, selecting equipment, training operators, converting storage media — all these mitigate against rapid change. Even if technology drops in price, the chances are the machine will continue to meet your needs for from three to five years. At the end of that period, if you want to trade in purchased equipment, you can even recover some of your costs. There is a lively market for used equipment. Instead of paying 10% of original value to own a machine you have leased for three years, you can sell it to someone else for 15% of its initial cost.

There are, of course, valid reasons for choosing rental or lease instead of purchase. Protection from obsolescence is not one of them. The relative merits of these three acquisition methods are described below.

Rental

Good for short (12 months or less) or uncertain needs; requires no major capital outlay. Rentals are treated as operating expenses, and are fully tax deductible. On the minus side, rentals build no equity. They offer no inflation protection. Not only that, but the cost per month is higher than for any other method. Some vendors will credit rental costs toward lease or purchase after a trial period.

Lease

Three to five years are common lengths of leases. Like rentals, leases require no major capital outlay. Thus, they are much easier on cash flow than purchases. This is their principal advantage. Leases that result in purchase must be capitalized. Some U.S. vendors pass investment tax credits through to customers; others retain them. Because payments are fixed, leases do offer some inflation protection. They are less expensive than rental, but more costly than purchase.

Purchase

Ideal for long-term usage. This acquisition method does require a large outlay of money. Purchases must be capitalized. All investment tax credits belong to the purchaser, who has full equity of ownership. Purchase results in the lowest monthly cost. However, buyers must take into account other potential uses for the money before deciding purchase is best.

9

Equipment Evaluation Criteria

At last, hardware and software! This chapter is all about equipment. It contains a set of evaluation criteria for just about everything that word processors can do. The criteria are carefully set up to help you check out the vendor, the hardware and the programs and capabilities.

Use these criteria to form the basis for your specification. Be selective. You may decide not to specify automatic carriage return, since all but a few electronic typewriters offer this feature. Unless you plan to use a feature like telecommunications, exclude that too. Choose everything you need, not everything you can.

In addition to listing the functions of word processing, the use of each is explained. Good and bad features to look for are pointed out. When you write your own specification, include as much detail as you need to make sure the vendor's answer is responsive.

Before we begin, let me say a word of appreciation to the *Seybold Report on Office Systems.* This newsletter is an excellent source of technical information (see publications list at the back of the book for address). I draw on this resource in my consulting practice. The way I have organized my evaluation criteria reflects the *Seybold Report* influence, and I acknowledge a professional debt.

KNOW YOUR VENDOR

Company Profile

Take a look at the manufacturer's track record. *Fortune* and other business magazines publish articles about market share and profitability. Try to pick a vendor who will stay around for five years.

Alistair Cooke, when asked to sum up the U.S. Civil War in a single sentence, was to the point: "The South had the audacity, but the North had the reserves." The same can be said for word processing companies. Small, innovative companies typically have the edge on technology. But the big name manufacturers have the capital for sustained research and service operations.

Some small companies have done quite well. Likewise, some major names have not been able to make money in WP. There are no hard and fast rules. A safe pick is a company that offers regular updates to a good line of equipment. This means they are committed to keeping up-to-date with changing technology.

Range of Products

If you start small, say with a non-display machine, you may be very concerned about obsolescence. What happens when you outgrow your machine? Must you start over again? Not always. Many vendors offer a range of systems starting with electronic typewriters and going the full route to shared-resource systems.

There are some important questions to ask: Are the machines truly compatible? Can you take a diskette from one machine and read it on the other? Does this work both ways? (In other words, can you go from blind machine to VDT and *back*?) Is telecommunications the only way in which these machines will "talk" to each other? How well do the various machines relate to each other in terms of features and capabilities?

Some vendors also offer different levels of software on a single system. Thus, you only pay for what you need. This is another good way to protect against obsolescence, but it requires more discipline. It's hard to resist buying the works when it's just "a little bit more."

Futures

Don't buy them. If they are announced (demonstrated at a trade show) and are not yet available in your area, they may be worth considering, (although you do well to doubt the promised local timetable).

If they are not yet available anywhere, be very careful. The manufacturer will probably deliver, but the typical timetable is very unreliable. Even for a current product line, you should inquire about delivery times. They range from 30 to 120 days. You should know how long you will have to wait.

Training

There has been a major shift in manufacturers' training policies in recent years. The trend is away from personal training provided by a marketing support representative (MSR) to self-guided training. This is provided through manuals, and audio-visual packages combining instructional cassettes and exercises on special floppy diskettes. Often, these self-paced packages are supplemented with some MSR support, or by an 800-number that can be called for quick assistance.

The manufacturers' rationale is two-fold. One, MSR training is too expensive to provide given the large number of WP machines now installed. Two, today's systems are easier to use and thus to set up as self-teaching machines. To the extent that manufacturers are passing cost savings on to the users, and they generally are, this is a legitimate assumption. It does, however, require extra care in evaluating how easily your typists will be able to learn new equipment.

In assessing vendors' training plans, three principles should guide your choice. First, the more MSR training the better. It is human nature to prefer personal instruction, and people respond most rapidly to it. Second, the manuals should be clear, concise and well-indexed. You should be able to go directly to a specific operation without having to thumb through pages of text. Don't forget, you and your typists will be referring to the manual long after the initial training is over. Third, the entire package should be self-paced. It will take a novice operator longer to learn a new machine than it will an experienced person who is simply switching machines. The typist with previous WP training should be able to skip some or all of the basic material without losing the gist of the training.

Evaluating the quality of training, therefore, is very important. Some of the more important questions to ask include:

(a) How many operators are trained per workstation? Ideally, it should be two.

(b) Where is training performed? Is it on site or at the vendor's office? The vendor's office usually means better facilities. Ask to train on your own applications, however.

(c) How is the training provided? Is it done by MSR or self-training manuals, or cassettes, or some combination?

(d) How long does the training take? And how much MSR time is provided for each operator trained?

(e) Are self-instruction manuals and cassettes available, and at what cost?

(f) Will the vendor provide training for all software updates?

(g) What is the cost of training additional operators?

Maintenance

Maintenance contracts are available from the manufacturers. They typically run from 1% to 1.5% of the purchase price per month. They aren't cheap.

For the most part, maintenance contracts are recommended. The equipment is sensitive and complex. It is not practical for customers to stock spare parts. However, maintenance is one item where you do not always get what you pay for. Evaluate the local representative's maintenance record:

(a) What is the average response time to service calls? Vendors keep these records; ask to see them.

(b) Will the vendor commit to four-hour response to service calls? The time could be more, or less, depending upon your needs. Sometimes you can negotiate a different rate for different response times.

(c) Where is the service staff based, and how large is it? Two persons in a city 100 miles away is not very reassuring.

(d) Is there a local source of parts inventories?

(e) What preventive maintenance is included in the contract? If all you get is response to actual problems, it may be cheaper to pay for service as you use it.

(f) Is there a 24-hour 800-number or other provision for assistance during night shifts and weekends?

(g) Does the machine offer self-diagnostic technology? Some machines run a special program to tell the service representative what's wrong with them. This usually makes for shorter service calls.

(h) Will the vendor rebate maintenance charges for poor performance? Some vendors will rebate 1/30th of the monthly maintenance for each day the machine is down. If you own the machine, this may be your only leverage to bargain for good service.

If you buy at the very low end of the market, service contracts may not be available. Typically, retail computer outlets cut their prices this way. You take your machine in when it breaks down and pick it up in two days or two weeks — however long it takes. However, some careful shoppers make this work for them. Do-it-yourself machines are so much cheaper that users can afford to buy a spare; they still spend less than for a standard word processor and contract.

Local Support

No matter how good a word processor looks on paper, your success is bound up with the quality of support from the local representative or distributor. Just as you check out the manufacturer's standing, so you should check out the reputation of the local office.

Ask for a complete list of users in your service area. Follow up on this list with personal inquiries. Contact local users or professional groups; members are often willing to share their experiences. Don't let one bad report throw you off. Get a representative sampling.

FOCUSING YOUR SELECTION

The first step in writing a specification is to decide on the level of equipment you want. Use the questions below to orient yourself to a category of equipment. Within a category, you should also think in terms of a level of capability. For example, do you want to edit long documents, sort large lists, and equip six typists now and four more next year? In that case, you will need a system with a hefty amount of storage and enough computer capacity to grow with you.

If you plan a large system, include workload statistics as well as the projected number of workstations and printers in your specification. Let the vendors propose their best shot at meeting your performance requirements. Sometimes they can make do with fewer units and still meet your needs. You may find this nets you a very attractive price.

Category of Equipment

Choose electronic typewriter, blind machine, VDT, stand-alone, or shared-resource. Or some combination. Allow the vendor as much flexibility as possible.

Microprocessors

Type

Not all microprocessors or "computer chips" are alike. Some are faster, larger and more efficient than others. This is a rapidly evolving technology. Trade publications and professional associations can help you keep abreast of changes. It is worthwhile knowing what microprocessor is used in a particular system. Make sure the system you are considering uses current technology. Some manufacturers are using 16-bit rather than 8-bit microprocessors for their systems. This means that their systems have a greater processing capacity and are generally more efficient.

Size

In addition to type, you will want to know how large each microprocessor is. A 32k microprocessor has 32,000 characters of memory; a 96k microprocessor has 96,000 and so on. The larger the computer, the larger the WP program it can handle — and the more efficient it will be.

Number

Most word and data processing systems have a single computer. However, some innovative manufacturers are beginning to incorporate a spare computer in every machine. This is a direct benefit of the drop in cost of computer logic. The advantage is that when one computer fails, the other automatically takes over. This is called redundancy, and it is an excellent way to protect yourself against systems failure. The cost for this extra protection is often quite reasonable.

Memory: ROM/RAM

Microprocessors have two kinds of memory: ROM (read only memory) and RAM (random access memory). ROM is permanent; programs stored in ROM can only be changed by changing the chip. Typically, the processor's operating system is stored in ROM. RAM memory can be changed by changing a diskette. Most machines use some combination of both. As a general rule, the more RAM the better.

Loading

In small systems, such as electronic typewriters, the program typically stays in the system. In stand-alone and some shared-resource systems, the program is stored on a diskette. Every time you turn the machine on you put the program in. Obviously, this makes it easy to change programs. But there are some potential problems you should ask about:

Is the entire program in memory at once? Often, the program is larger than the memory. This means that you leave the program diskette in the machine at all times. The machine selects the right parts of the program depending upon what you are doing. However, if your system has limited diskette capacity, you are giving up working document storage. You won't have this problem if you can remove the software diskette after loading.

Is the entire program on a single diskette? (Switching diskettes to go from editing to list processing, for example, is awkward.) If you are using hard disks, be sure to ask how much space your programs will use up, and how much working storage you will have.

Shared-Resource Management

There are a number of ways in which WP systems share resources. Stand-alones can share printers, workstations can share a computer, or workstations can have their own computers and simply share disk storage. The latter two options are usually called shared-resource systems. If you are considering anything more complex than sharing a printer between two stand-alone workstations, there are some questions you should ask:

Is the computer logic centralized or distributed to the workstations? The latter option is called distributed logic. As a general rule — and general applies more than rule — there are some advantages to distributed logic. The system is not vulnerable to failure of the central computer, since each workstation has its own.

However, distributed logic systems do require a central controller — sort of an electronic traffic cop — to control information going to and from storage and the workstations and printers. If the controller or the storage fails, the entire system will still be out of commission.

What is the maximum allowable distance between components of the system? Usually, after 1,000 feet or more, the efficiency of the machines drops off. For instance, the screen display must "refresh" the image at a certain rate to avoid flicker. More than 1,000 feet, and there may be problems. You can always link distant components using a telecommunications link, but you will pay more to do it (see chapter 13).

At what point will degradation occur? Degradation means that the system slows down because too many concurrent demands are being made of it. For instance, repagination and list processing are both heavy users of computer capacity. If two typists run these simultaneously, the system may respond sluggishly. The screens will display information very slowly. It is difficult to get a reliable answer to this question, but it is worth probing for. Ask to see concurrent operations on large files in a demonstration.

How do terminals access and share disk storage? If all terminals share a single disk, the system is more likely to slow up. However, if there are several disks, you want to be sure that these are not rigidly assigned to specific workstations. In other words, terminal A may usually record on disk A. However, terminal A should be able to edit a large procedures manual stored by another typist on disk B. The typists should be able to work with documents by name without having to keep track of which disk they are on. The system should remember that for them. Some newer systems even allow you to recall documents using words occurring in the text. You can bypass the index altogether.

Can independent terminals be linked to the system? An independent terminal has its own microprocessor and its own data storage. It is, in effect, a stand-alone unit. When linked to a shared-resource system, it has access to documents stored on the system. This option has two advantages. If the main system fails, you have something to fall back on. For remote users, it may be easier to make them independent for most operations, linking them only when information is shared. Otherwise, coordinating document filing gets complicated.

Can several systems be linked together? There are special communications, called local area networks packages that link several stand-alone or even shared-resource systems together. These special packages go a step farther than traditional telecommunications. They allow operators to work with documents anywhere in the system, without knowing where the documents are stored. Thus, you can have two shared-resource systems which look like a single unit to the typists at their workstations. This distributes the load, reducing the risk of degradation.

It also means that if one unit fails, you are still able to operate. There is no central controller upon which all units depend. The most sophisticated of these communications networks allows you to incorporate several vendors' WP equipment in a single network, as well as linking up with photocomposers, computers and intelligent copiers and printers.

Multifunction Capabilities

A mouthful, that one, but not nearly as confusing as the industry terms: foreground/background and transparency.

Foreground/Background

Foreground means you tie up the system, whether blind, stand-alone or shared-resource, to complete some task. For example, inputting and editing a document are foreground operations. The screen and/or keyboard is dedicated to that function exclusively.

Background means simultaneous operations. While some foreground operation is in process a background operation, such as assembling documents, is being done at the same time. The advantage, of course, is the increased efficiency of the machine. Questions to ask include:

Can any text editing functions, such as merging address lists and letters, be done in background? Can printing be done in background? VDTs do this by definition.

Can communications be handled in background? This means you can send a document to a remote location, such as from field to headquarters, while still using the word processor for foreground operations. Not many machines can do this. However, telecommunications are so fast that the interruption is no problem for infrequent users.

Can OCR input be handled in background? (For a full explanation of optical character readers, see chapter 11.) Many OCR readers are hard-wired directly to the word processor. They record the text they scan directly on the word processor's disk. Some machines do this in foreground, meaning the word processor is tied up until the scanning is done. Others do this is in background. If you are planning to use OCR, look for background operation.

A word of caution about personal computers: keyboarding and printing may not be true simultaneous operations. While in theory these systems offer background printing, in practice some of the systems degrade so badly that it is not practical. The problem is less a function of hardware than of inefficient operating systems. If you are planning to use a personal computer for word processing, check out this feature carefully.

Transparency

Transparent operations means you have access to both word processing programs and data processing programs at the same time. More simply put, word and data processing look like one big program to the typist.

Transparency is only an issue if you are planning to use your word processor for data processing as well. (Chapter 10 provides a full explanation.) What it means is that records created as part of data processing operations can be edited with word processing and vice versa.

It sounds more complicated than it is, so let's look at an example. An office supply firm has a WP/DP system. Accounts payable maintains a file of all sales as part of the data processing program. This is used to generate invoices, post payments, and age past-due accounts.

In a given month, the summary report indicates 58 customers' accounts are more than 60 days old. This is an unusual situation, so the office manager decides to send some personalized, friendly reminders.

What the manager wants to do is pull the name, address, item, date of purchase and amount due from the payables file and merge this information with a repetitive letter. In a transparent system, the typist can extract the necessary information and then generate the letters using word processing. If WP and DP are not transparent, the exchange will be awkward at best. Different software diskettes are loaded to run word processing and data processing. Moving information between them is difficult.

Most systems that offer both DP and WP are not transparent. You will have to decide how great a disadvantage this is, based on your knowledge of your own workload. The tradeoff, if you want transparency, is limiting your choice to a system which you might not choose otherwise.

Minimum/Maximum Configuration

In deciding on a level of equipment for today, you also should think about future growth. To some extent, this is covered by selecting a vendor who offers a range of products as discussed above. But even a single system can be set up in different ways. It is useful to know the minimum and maximum configuration it will carry. Details for evaluating workstations and storage are addressed later in this chapter. However, for the purpose of orienting yourself to the right level of equipment, you should consider these preliminary questions:

What is the minimum/maximum number of workstations and printers shared by stand-alone units? Some allow two or three workstations per printer or two printers per workstation.

What is the minimum/maximum number of workstations and printers supported by a shared-resource system? Usually, these are lumped together as peripherals. There is a maximum number of peripherals, but you can mix them any way you want.

What is the minimum/maximum data storage capacity? It used to be that this was a question for shared-resource system machines only. Stand-alones had an upper limit of two diskettes or about 250 pages total. Today, even small systems can use hard disks with storage of 5,000 pages or more. Knowing the maximum available storage is very useful for planning.

Other Add-ons

If you need telecommunications, OCR, photocomposition or data processing, this will affect the kind of systems you should consider. Think about expanded uses of your system early.

HARDWARE COMPONENTS

Storage

Before we get to storage specifications, a brief review of the possibilities is in order. To oversimplify a bit, storage media come in three shapes: tapes, cards and disks. Tapes and, to some extent, cards are serial — or sequential — media. You work with text in the order it is on the media. There are lots of machines still around which use tapes and cards. Nevertheless, they are an obsolete technology, and are not discussed further here.

Disk Characteristics

Disks are round. They permit random access to any point on the media. Information is stored on tracks and sectors, which the system uses as an address for retrieving text. Information can be stored out of order, which makes it easy to insert more after the first draft. Only the machines needs to know where it is.

Disks are also fast. Disks are described as floppy diskettes (often called diskettes or even floppies for short) if they are handled in a flexible paper protective jacket. If sealed in a plastic container, they are called hard disks. (See Figure 9.1.)

Diskettes come in several sizes: 5¼-inch and 8-inch are the most common. Diskettes used to store about 256K (thousand) characters per side. Only one side was recorded. Thus, a diskette held about 125 pages and was called single-density (1D), single-sided (1S). Today diskettes are being packed 1D-2S, and 2D-2S. In the last configuration, a single super-diskette holds one MB (megabyte, or million characters). Furthermore, there are now 8-inch hard disks that store 10 MB (or roughly 5,000 pages) in the same space that the old diskettes used for 125 pages.

Disk Storage

Hard disks are traditionally 14 inches in diameter. Hard disk storage is expressed two ways. There is fixed disk storage, which always stays in the system. Removable disk storage allows you to change some of the platters (as disks are sometimes called). This means you can copy information from the fixed disk and store it offline. Otherwise, once you filled the disk up, you couldn't add any new documents. Some systems without removable disks use diskettes to copy for offline storage. This method is not preferred, because so many diskettes are needed per disk.

Diskettes and disks are mounted on drives. The old 1D-1S diskettes rotated at five or six revolutions per second. The new 8-inch disks spin at 52 revolutions per second. The 14-inch hard disks are even faster. Thus not only can you store more data, but you can get to it faster.

Finally, bubble memory and other technologies are pushing against hard disk technology for a place in the market. All of these developments are changing the rules. It is no longer possible to assume that a stand-alone machine uses diskettes or that a hard disk machine implies a big shared-resource system. In fact, a small office with a large file of information now has access to reasonably-priced equipment that can operate at what used to be computer performance standards.

Figure 9.1 Diagram of Diskette and Disk Pack

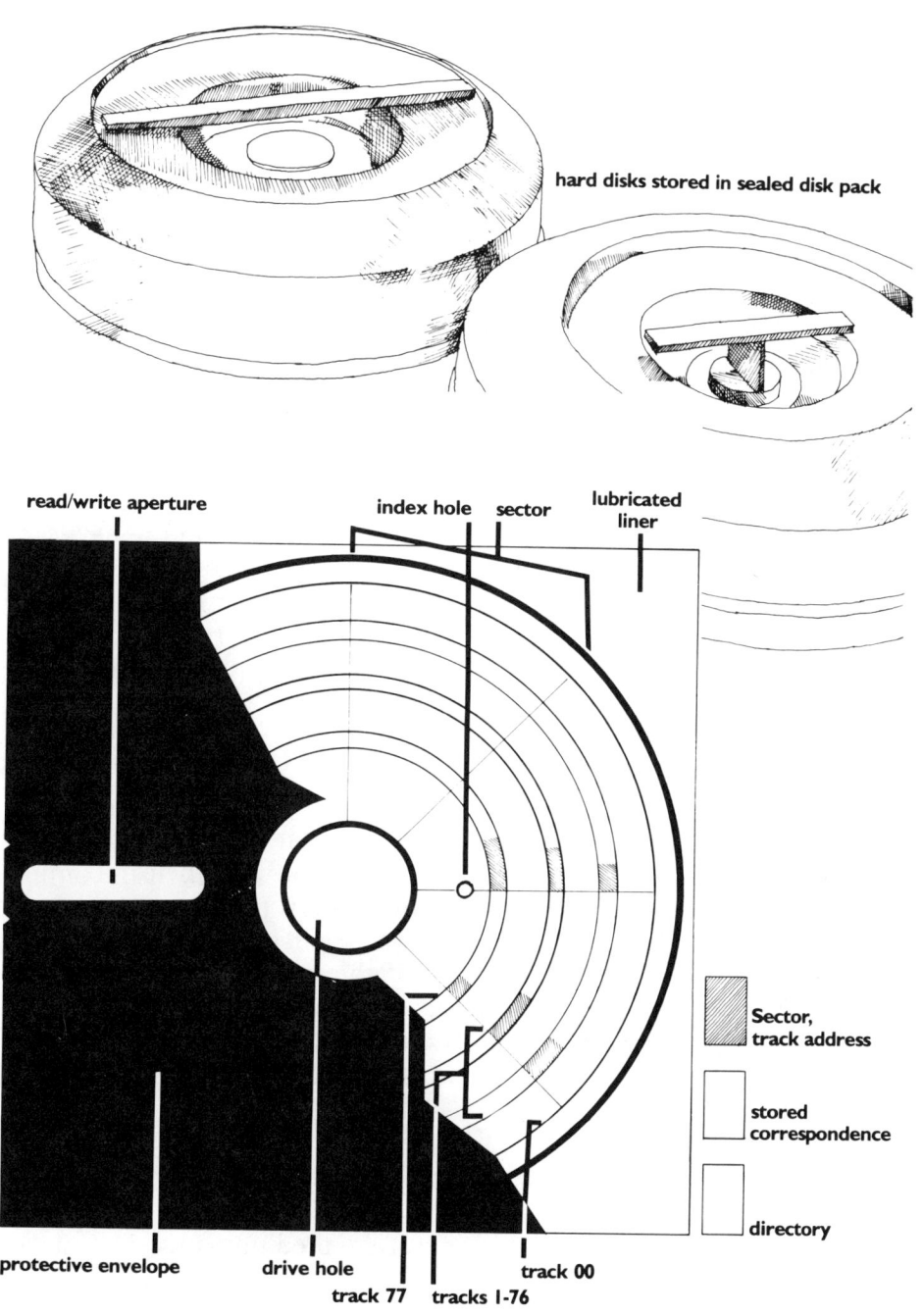

Source: Courtesy of Word Processing Systems

Evaluating Storage Capability

How, then, to evaluate storage on a system? What you really need to know is how much you get, how fast you can access it, and what limits are imposed on file size.

For instance, even with a hard disk system, you may be limited to a certain number of documents per platter. If you have a large list processing application, you may not be able to sort files *across* disk drives. For instance, you might have two 5 MB disks on separate drives. Your file requires 6 MB of storage. You have it in alphabetical order and want to reorder it in customer number order. However, the program doesn't allow you to take records from drives A and B and merge them into a new order. You can sort A and B separately, but that doesn't really give you an integrated file.

Not only that, if you have a 6 MB file, you will need at least 6 MB of working storage or "scratch pad." The system uses this in sorting. What it does is leave the master file intact and copy the records in the new order in working storage. Thus, for a short time, you have two files. And you still need enough storage for all of your on-going WP programs and applications. Many users of hard disk systems severely underestimate the rate at which storage accumulates, particularly when shared by several typists. It is always wise to buy as much storage as you can reasonably afford.

Writing a Specification

Keeping all this in mind, then, how do you write a specification for storage? Figure out the maximum number of records and their maximum total length. Convert this to the amount of characters or pages you will need online at one time. (You will, of course, have more files stored offline, but that doesn't really count toward the capacity of the system.) From this, either you or the vendor can work up the actual requirement for diskette or disk capacity. Don't forget to leave enough "scratch pad" space. Allowing the vendor flexibility in terms of providing a super-diskette or a hard disk often pays off with larger systems.

Your storage specification should take the following into account:

Storage Medium — What unit storage medium is used? Is it 1D-1S diskette, 8-inch sealed disk, or what?

Maximum Characters — What is the maximum number of characters per drive? Is this a 256K diskette or a 24 MB hard disk? You will want to know the current amount of online (in the system) storage being proposed, as well as the absolute maximum to which you can expand.

How much of this storage medium is dedicated to systems functions? In smaller systems with two diskette drives, the WP program may take up most of one of the diskettes. If this system diskette must remain on the system at all times, the net working storage may not be enough. Even hard disk systems give up substantial space to program storage.

Maximum Documents — What is the maximum number of documents into which each storage unit can be divided? Is that 4 MB disk limited to 2,000 separate documents? If so, and if you have 3,000 short documents, you will have to pack them on two disks instead of one. This is not an efficient use of storage.

File Size — What is the largest file of documents and characters that can be handled as a unit? If you have a large document, such as an engineering specification, or if you plan extensive list processing, this is very important.

Hard Disk — If hard disk will be used, how much is fixed and how much removable? If all the disk is fixed, what provision is made for copying files?

Speed of Copying — How long does it take to copy a diskette or disk?

Speed of Access — How long does it take to get access to a particular record in a full diskette or disk? How long to sort your complete list processing file? Answers to these questions tell you how responsive your system will be. It is more meaningful than asking how many diskette rotations per second. For example, you might specify that a system should sort 5,000 records of 100 characters each in 45 minutes or less.

Vulnerability — How are files recovered after interrupted editing? How does the system handle changes during editing? Are two documents created, one altered and one not? If a power failure occurs when editing is almost complete are all changes lost? What is the maximum amount of text that can be lost due to power or systems failure? Does the machine have a built-in battery to keep the information in working storage intact during short power failures? For how long?

By asking all these questions, perhaps during a demonstration, you can get a feel for the vulnerability of your system. Power fluctuations and failures are real problems for material in the buffer (working storage). Text recorded on the diskette or disk is safer, unless the read-write head "crashes." That unfriendly term means that the information recorded on the diskette is accidentally destroyed by the device used to read it in and out of the machine's memory.

Security — How does the system provide for file security? In a diskette-based system, security is usually provided by locking up the diskette. In a rigid disk system, of course, this isn't practical. You may have several hundred documents on line at a given time, representing many authors' and typists' work. In this environment, certain documents are assigned passwords; only those who know the passwords can have access to the documents. Some systems even offer two or three levels of passwords. A nice feature is to be able to change the password for all documents in a file at a single command.

Error Correction — Does the disk controller use an error correction code? If a high-speed disk is densely packed, the possibility for read-write errors goes up. Some vendors have technology that deals with this problem.

Displays

There are two kinds of displays: thin windows and page displays. Thin windows vary from a few characters to a single line. They provide a "window into memory," to use a vendor's apt term. You can check visually that a character is recorded or changed correctly.

Thin windows permit electronic typewriters to handle proportional and justified printing, something that used to be the exclusive province of VDT word processors. However, character and line displays do *not* permit simultaneous input and output. As such, machines that use this technology are still classified here as non-display machines. This is not to say that blind machines do not have their place. They most certainly do. But they do not belong in a discussion of display technology. The rest of this section pertains to word processors whose displays, however large or small, permit simultaneous keyboarding and printing.

Displays range in size from about seven lines up to two full pages of text. The more display, the more money the system costs — usually. As with everything else, at any given time an innovative vendor may challenge traditional price barriers. In evaluating displays, there are many factors to keep in mind.

Physical Characteristics

What is the physical configuration of the display?

Color of Background and Characters — Varying combinations of green and white through black. Full color screens, as they become economical, will be more attractive for all-day viewing. Some displays allow operators to reverse the image and background colors, which is nice.

Composition of Characters — Dot matrix and height of letters. In cathode ray tubes, characters are composed by a dot matrix, 7 x 9, 9 x 15, or whatever. Larger numbers usually mean sharper images. Larger-size letters on a screen are also easier to read. Some professional workstations use a technology called bit-mapping. This allows the system to plot out a very precise image through a dot by dot technique. It also gives much more variety in displaying symbols, diagrams, etc.

Number of Characters Per Line — How many will display and how many will print?

Number of Lines Per Screen — Status lines and text. Status lines give a visual indication of margins, tabs and the current line position on the page. In some systems, status indicators remain on the screen at all times; others display them only on command. Partial- and full-page text displays are both acceptable.

Dual Page or Split Screen Capability — Two different pages of text displayed. This is useful for comparing a master document with an edited version, or to view source data while composing a document. Some systems allow four "windows" per screen.

Special Magnify Modes — Double-size letters or preview of page format. Double-size display of letters reduces the amount of text on the screen, but has the opposite effect on the operator's willingness to look at it. Word processors with partial-page displays sometimes offer a preview option. This shows the typist a block diagram of the text as it will fill the page. If necessary, format can then be adjusted.

Ease of Use

How easy is the display to use?

Tiltable Display — Adjusts to different angles.

Movable Display or Keyboard — Adjusts to different positions. This is a real plus for comfort. Usually, the keyboard and display will be connected by a cable rather than molded as a single unit.

Logical Layout — Placement of function keys and cursor. Frequently used keys are best placed to the right and left of "home" row. Other keys should be on top. The whole setup should make sense.

Touch — How comfortable. This is a matter of personal taste.

10-Key Pad — Allows number typing with right hand only, for long streams of numeric typing. Of course, the number keys are still in their regular place as well.

Cursor Positioning — How achieved? Some machines use five keys, one for each direction, plus home. Others are pressure-sensitive to a direction. Some cursors move freely, while others move by text increment only. There are also machines that move the text rather than the cursor up and down the screen. All typing is done on the "home" line. The choice is largely a matter of personal preference.

Scrolling — Horizontal and vertical. Scrolling moves text up and down or across the screen. Vertical scrolling allows the typist to scan all text as if on a continuous sheet of paper. Horizontal scrolling displays print lines which exceed the character width of the screen. Scrolling can be continuous or it can jump a screenful at a time. The former method is usually preferred.

Menus — Lists of operator commands. A menu is a displayed list of functions which a VDT word processor is ready to perform. For instance, a start-up menu asks if you want to create a new document, edit an old one, or print, etc. By choosing one option, you may get another menu. Creating a new document will cause the machine to ask you for a name and format. Menus are very useful for new users, but experienced operators should be able to free themselves from this procedure.

Glare Reduction — How accomplished and how effective?

Accuracy of Display

How accurately does the display represent text?

Pitch — Variable or mono spacing. Many machines display the same number of characters per inch, or pitch, regardless of how the document will print. Thus, the typist cannot fine tune the format on the screen. This defeats the purpose of WP. When you get to proportional spacing, you have real problems. Because of the variable space per letter, a monospaced line ending on the screen may not coincide with the printed line. Systems with proportional displays are rare. However, some machines do keep track of line endings to ensure that display line and print line endings match.

Underlining — Single, double and vertical. Some machines display a code which tells the typist that underlining has been entered, but it does not display on the screen. Display of the actual underscoring is easier to work with. Vertical and horizontal lines which can be used to print graphs and charts are also very handy.

Subscripts and Superscripts — Numbers and letters. Again, display of characters rather than codes is preferred.

Justified Text Display — Single and dual column.

Highlighting — Extra intensity display of text between two cursor-defined positions. For moving or deleting, this feature is used to verify that the right amount of text is involved.

Extra Character Sets — Display of foreign languages, technical symbols and special characters.

Output

Output means getting from display and diskette to printed copy. In the true sense of the word, it also refers to using telecommunications to transmit a final document to another system. Finally, it can refer to output to a photocomposer, intelligent copier, or other office machine. These we will deal with in later chapters. For now, let's concentrate on printers.

Printer technology has been changing. But printers have remained relatively expensive compared to the word processors they support. In part, this is due to the fact that printing is more or less a mechanical function. This imposes some inherent limitations. Very recently, however, the ground rules have begun to change. First of all, price barriers for letter quality printers are breaking. And secondly, completely new technologies are being used.

Impact vs. Non-impact Printing

Traditional printing technology is impact printing. One way or another, something strikes the paper and leaves a mark. Most impact printers use character printers. Fully formed characters conforming to a particular typeface are mounted on a daisy wheel or other device.

Line printers are another kind of impact printer. They use dot matrices or other methods to compose a standard character. They do not permit varying typefaces, nor are they final quality. Line printers are, however, much faster.

Character printers produce about 15 to 75 characters per second (cps). Line printers produce anywhere from 120 to 300+ lines per minute (lpm). At roughly 70 characters per line, this means about 100 to 300 cps. Line printers cost more, but you need fewer of them. They are ideal for speeding drafts back to authors, but not for writing letters to your best customers.

Non-impact printers are still quite new. The ink jet printer is an early entry. It sprays charged droplets on paper. It is only marginally faster than character printers and is likely to be passed by.

Image Printers

More promising are image printers. These combine either fiber optics or lasers with plain paper copier technology. Essentially, these machines compose an image of the information stored on a diskette and print that image on paper — usually a page at a time. For those of you familiar with computer output microfilm (COM), the concept (but not the process) is the same. COM translates computer tapes or disks to microfilm. Image printers translate WP diskettes or disks to paper.

Image printers offer several advantages. They are fast, producing as many as 36 to 75 or more pages per minute. (This is as much as 1,200 to 2,000 cps.) More importantly, because they are truly electronic printers, they can provide software to vary both the typeface and size of characters on a single page — without running the page several times.

Image printers are expensive. Often they cost 10 or more times as much as a character printer. However, not only do you need fewer of them, but they also double as computer printers. (Character printers are much too slow to keep up with the volume.) Finally, because they work with digital information, it is possible to combine both text and computerized data, such as graphs and charts, in a single document.

In a sense, image printers perform the same function as photocomposers: enhancing the appearance of text with a variety of typefaces and sizes. At present, image printers do not offer the same crisp quality. They are not up to camera-ready copy for reproduction. However, as the technology improves — and it likely will — image printers should give photocomposers a good run for the money.

Intelligent Copiers

Another output technology to consider is intelligent copiers. These machines link a word processor to an office copier that can accept both digital and hard-copy paper input. Intelligent copiers differ from image printers in their ability to function as traditional office copy machines when not being used for word processing. Both types of machines excel at producing multiple, collated sets. Some intelligent copiers cost as little as an electronic typewriter, but to get good image quality you must pay much more.

Choosing Printers

In choosing printers for your own operation, you want to make sure you have enough to keep up with your typists and authors. Turnaround of typed documents should not be delayed for printing. Neither should expensive printers be allowed to sit idle for much of the time. Finally, you must take into account the need for finished or draft quality. Typically, you will need about half as many impact printers as typists — depending upon physical placement and the mix of character printers and high-speed printers. One image printer can support 10 or more typists. In evaluating printers, aside from the paramount issue of price, you should evaluate the following:

Type of Printers Available — Plan for growth. Not all word processors offer other than character printers.

Speed — Remember a line is 70 characters more or less. An average page is about 2,000 characters, a full page is about 3,900 characters.

Character Sets — This is less a question of how many sets are offered than of how many characters per set. Unless you want a very special typeface, which you should ask about, most printers support a wide variety of interchangeable typing elements. However, if you want to add special characters, such as Greek letters for scientific notation, you must look more closely. It used to be that you had to run the page twice, once for each character set. Then there were machines which handled two daisy wheels at once. More expensive, but a lot less hassle. Now there are machines that will handle vastly expanded character sets on a single typing element. If you are thinking of an image printer, ask also how many styles and sizes are online (available for use without interrupting the system) at the same time.

Sharing of Printers — For stand-alone machines, you want to make sure two or more input stations can use the same printer. Physically transferring diskettes from machine to machine doesn't count.

Printer Queuing — If several machines share a printer, the system will normally print documents in the order received. Make sure you can override this order to print high priority documents. You should also be able to group a set of documents which will be printed on the same stationery.

Automatic Paper Handling — Most printers handle continuous paper using a forms tractor. Automatic sheet and envelope feeds try to accomplish the same thing — no manual feeding of each page — without the awkward problem of using continuous paper. They do this with mixed success. Ask for references who use the sheet feed proposed by your vendor. As a rule, single-sheet feeds are more reliable than duals. If you plan to use a sheet feed, ask about paper weight and size limitations. Will it handle a carbon set?

File Note Typing — Sometimes called typewriter mode, this means being able to bypass the display and type directly on a document. The most common use is the typing of carbon copy notes which should not appear on the original.

Bold Overprinting — This automatically double-prints a given character string. It darkens or highlights the text, and has the same effect as underlining.

SOFTWARE COMPONENTS

Indexing and Filing

A diskette or disk is basically a compact filing cabinet. The word processor labels and files documents in much the same way as you would in a paper file. There are, however, two significant differences. First, not all pieces of the same document have to be physically located together. The word processor's program keeps track of where they are. And second, you can't see where the machine has put them.

For this reason, you are very dependent upon the WP system's document indexing and retrieval capabilities. You want a means of knowing what's in storage, how old various documents are, and what belongs to which typist and which author. You also want to be sure that you are working with the right edition of a document that has gone through multiple revisions. All of this is lumped together as document indexing and file management. Some of the things to look for:

Structure — What is the structure of the index? Some systems number documents, which is not as easy to reference as naming them. The number of characters allowed for the name also varies; the more the better.

Sub-sets — Can sub-sets of the index be set up? Sophisticated systems allow you to generate indexes by author or typist, regardless of placement on the disk. Others allow you to build a working index or file of very active documents, so that you don't have to sort through an entire index every time you want to use them.

Global Indexes — Can global indexes be set up? Even some diskette-based systems let you create an index of everything stored on media, whether online or offline. Thus, you can build a complete index of an author's work.

Document Histories — How does the system handle document histories? The index ideally should tell you how long the document is, when it was created, when last edited, when last printed, for whom, and by which typist. Some document histories also tell you what format or special instructions have been set up for each document.

Productivity — Does the system provide productivity information? This indicates the number of keystrokes or lines involved, and sometimes the elapsed keyboard time as well. These statistics are handy for checking input productivity. They are not as meaningful during editing. The system still reports total lines, whereas only those that changed are important. Depending on the complexity of the changes, time spent on the machine is also a poor measure of editing productivity.

Formatting

Not to belabor a point, but formatting is a large part of what word processing is all about. It's not just what you print, but how you print. The placement of text on a page, the ability to work within the constraints of a form, the addition of proportional spacing and justified columns — all these come under the general heading of formatting.

A good word processing system should be judged on the range of formatting features it offers and how simple these are to use. Evaluation criteria include:

Establishing Default and Unique Formats — These include pitch, spacing, margins, page lengths and tabs or indents. A default format is set up automatically if the typist does not specify anything else. This saves time when you use the same format over and over. Some systems have a built-in default format; others allow operators to establish their own. The latter is preferred. All systems permit unique formats to be set for specific documents, although some are easier to create than others.

Changing Formats — You should be able to set special formats — including odd-size pages — within a document. This is necessary to handle quotes, charts, listings or whatever. You should also be able to have justified and ragged text in a single document. If you have several similar documents, such as standard paragraphs or letters, you should be able to change the format of all of them at the same time. This is called a global format change.

Forms Formats — Most word processors allow you to store the tab and spacing settings needed to print a form. Thereafter, you can advance automatically from data element to data element with a single keystroke. Assuming your forms are consistently printed, the machine will fill in all the blanks correctly. You don't need a display machine to do this — some electronic typewriters handle forms quite well. If you do plan to use a VDT, you can look for one that displays a facsimile of the form on the screen.

Headers and Footers — A header — or footer — is a standard block of text carried on the top — or bottom — of each page. It might include the name of the addressee, the date and the page number. In this case, the header would start with the second page, and the page number would advance automatically from page to page. The typist should have complete flexibility in specifying the amount and placement of header/footer text. The system should also be able to alternate the placement on odd and even pages. This way, the information always falls on the outside margin if you have facing pages.

Automatic Numbering of Text — One of the most time-consuming tasks confronting a typist is outlined text. Whether a simple outline or a series of chapters, sections, paragraphs and sub-paragraphs, the problem is the same: the correct numbering sequence must be maintained at all times. At last, there are WP systems that do this automatically. Look for ones that allow maximum flexibility, handling upper and lower case letters and Roman and Arabic numbers.

Table of Contents/Indexes — Once a system has numbered or lettered certain blocks of text, it can pull all the headings together, list the page of occurrence, and create a table of contents or illustrations or whatever. The system can do the same thing with key words that you supply, such as a list of citations in a long legal document. The system alphabetizes your list, and for each term prints the pages on which it occurs. A painless cross-index is created.

Automatic Footnote Controls — In addition to numbering sections of text, WP software can also handle the numbering of footnotes through a long document. If you add or delete a note, the system automatically adjusts the affected numbers. In addition, a good system will ensure that the note in text and the reference *always* appear on the same page, no matter how much material you add or delete.

Auto-centering — You should be able to center a line or a page or an entire document. If you are typing dual columns, you should be able to center both columns automatically.

Widows and Orphans — Widow lines are single sentences at the top or bottom of a page — usually the result of a new paragraph. Good form says there should always be at least two lines. Auto widow line controls correct for this. You should also be able to specify that certain blocks of text, such as charts, are never split between two pages. Otherwise, you create orphans.

Columnar Typing — Most word processors align decimals automatically. You tab to the next column, type the number, and the system places it correctly. If you are typing a set of 100 numbers, you want a system that distributes the items evenly among as many columns as you set up. Ideally, if you add or delete numbers, the system should redistribute the columns again.

Complex Formats — You may have a special requirement, such as typing flow charts, diagrams, equations or foreign language text. Ask for an unrehearsed demonstration using examples of your own work. This is your best source of information about how well the system performs.

Editing

Editing can be as simple as reformatting a line or as complex as changing the order of every paragraph in a document. Formatting and editing are closely related. However, for our purposes, editing refers to a word processor's ability to change original input. Obviously, the hallmark of a good system is the ease with which this is accomplished. Look for maximum capability achieved with a minimum of keystrokes.

Pagination and Repagination — Once you tell the system how many lines to print per page, the rest should be automatic. During original input there is no problem. During editing, however, insertions and deletions may change page breaks. Look for systems that repage automatically, without your having to scan each change manually. Ideally, pagination should be a background operation.

Searching for Text — Before you can edit, you have to get to the right place in the stored text. Most systems today allow a character string search. In other words, you type in the characters which uniquely define the position you want, and the word processor puts you there.

It is also useful to be able to search by page number, by numbered or lettered text, or by a screen at a time. When using a system that moves a screen at a time, make sure you have the option of seeing the bottom of one screen and the top of the next together, if you wish. In other words, don't be limited to moving by complete screenfuls alone.

Insertions/Deletions — Ask how much text you can insert. Are you limited to a screen or a pageful? What if you want to incorporate another document, perhaps prepared in advance, in the middle of your current one? With regard to deletions, how do you define the text to be deleted? Some systems position the cursor fore and aft, which is cumbersome for short deletions. Others use a delete key and a separate key for character, word, sentence, line and paragraph. Ideally, you should be able to work both ways. Text to be deleted should be highlighted so that you can verify that it is correctly defined. To save you from inadvertent deletions, a double keystroke should be required.

Changes — The simplest changes are handled by overstrikes where one keystroke replaces another. Global changes, on the other hand, are more complex. A global change substitutes one character string for another throughout the document. For example, a misspelled name can be corrected or a title changed. There are a number of things to consider in evaluating global changes. How many characters can you match up? Somewhere between 17 and 30 characters is acceptable. How many separate changes can you make in a single pass through a document? If you want to make three or four global changes, you should be able to do this all at once. Do you have the option of reviewing each change? There may be some occurrences of the character string you want to save. You should be able to review each change or not, as you wish. Can you also tell the machine to ignore first caps and/or punctuation? Sometimes you will want to make changes regardless. Other times, a first cap or comma may alter the meaning of your character string, in which case you want the global change software to ignore it.

Block Copy/Move — A block of text can be anything you want — a column of numbers, several columns of numbers, a paragraph, or a page. You want to be able to move that block around freely, within the original or even to another document. You also want to have the option of deleting it from the first location, as well as leaving it there and recreating it somewhere else. This feature is very useful for assembling master paragraphs into a unique document. It is also used in statistical typing. One column is deleted, the rest shifted one column to the right, and the new current column is entered in the correct place.

Save Areas — When you move a block of text, you hold it in a save area while you switch from the old text position to the new. Ask how large these save areas are, and also how many there are. If a system offers multiple save areas, ask how these are indexed. You want to make sure you can find your way back easily.

Hyphenation/Spelling Dictionaries — A perfect hyphenation program probably does not exist. There are two relatively sound approaches. One makes hyphenation decisions automatically, but allows the operator to review each decision prior to printing. Essentially, the system does a global search — but not a change — for each hyphen. The other approach stores a hyphenation program based on standard rules of grammar. These are usually error-prone.

Spelling dictionaries are just beginning to be used to check hyphenation decisions. Their primary use, of course, is to protect us from typos and bad spellers. The best spelling programs are interactive, meaning that you can call the program in to check a part of a document and make the corrections on the spot. Batch programs run through the entire document each time, and only after the entire program has run can you view the flagged words and make changes.

Hallmarks of good spelling programs are the number of words they contain, the number of words you can add, and the speed with which the program runs. Another good feature of interactive spelling checkers is the ability to add a word to the dictionary as soon as the system flags it. In other words, if the machine stops at your name as a word it does not recognize, you should be able to add it to your permanent dictionary on the spot. Also, the program should recognize words that have been capitalized, punctuated, or hyphenated.

Revision Marks — Sometimes you want to mark changed text either on the display or on the printed copy. This helps you speed directly to the corrections during proofreading. Ask if and how the system you are considering accomplishes this. In legal documents, you may even need an audit trail. For example, a city may want to carry both stricken and revised text in a new version of an ordinance. Ask if and how your system handles this.

Document Assembly — This means selecting items from a set of prerecorded paragraphs, addresses, etc., to prepare one or more final documents. Ask how many prerecorded texts may be merged. Are you limited to two, such as a paragraph file and an address file, or can you select from several places? Can you enter keyboarded text as well? When you are working exclusively with prerecorded text, can the assembly and printing be handled as a background operation? Most importantly, can you save copies of the assembled documents after printing? Some systems delete these automatically.

SPECIAL APPLICATIONS

Without getting into true data processing, which is the subject of the next chapter, there are two gray areas we have talked about before: list processing and math processing. In addition, there are two other special applications to consider. These are called glossary functions and user-defined keys. Sometimes the terms are used interchangeably. However, it is important to understand each separately.

A glossary stores text which is likely to be used in a wide variety of documents. Each glossary term has a label or code by which it is retrieved. By tapping the glossary key and the right code, you insert the glossary text wherever you choose. If you have a long signature block, for example, you can record it under the author's initials. Whenever you need the signature block, the glossary re-enters it all for you. Some vendors even use glossaries to store standard paragraphs and addresses for document assembly.

A user-defined key (UDK) is closely related to a glossary. However, instead of storing text, it stores a procedure. If you perform some task over and over again, the system "remembers" the order in which the command keys are to be used.

For example, let's say each month you update a financial report. You delete the oldest month column, move the other 11 over, add a new one, and recompute year-to-date totals. Using a UDK, you can store this sequence of steps and use it over and over again each month. All you have to do is enter the new figures.

Doesn't this sound like programming? In a very real sense, it is. The only difference is that you are limited to combining the tasks the word processor already knows how to perform. You can't then ask it to compare this year's performance with last year's. That's still data processing. But it's getting very hard to tell WP and DP apart.

When the above applications are presented as part of standard or optional WP software, we will evaluate them as part of the WP system. In all cases, you must have a clear idea of what you really need. You can't evaluate the usefulness of these applications in a vacuum. Beyond that, you can organize your selection criteria as follows.

List Processing

In evaluating list processing software, it is important to keep in mind what it is and what it is not. List processing is designed to resequence records according to a variety of alphabetical and numeric instructions. It is also designed to compare these records against any preset value you specify, and tell you whether a given record's value is greater than, less than, or equal to the one you specified.

What list processing software cannot do is select two records or two fields within a record and compare them to each other. In other words, you cannot ask the system to look at actual sales and projected sales and tell you which is greater. This requires decision-making, and to date is only available with data processing software. However, limited decision processing may be incorporated in some list processing packages in the future. With this in mind, list processing evaluation criteria are as follows:

Minimum/Maximum — What is the minimum/maximum number of records online? Characters per record? Fields per record? If you have a very large record divided into 50 or 60 fields, can the system recognize and search for each field? Some systems limit the number of "key" fields on which a sort or select can be performed, even though the record can be divided into many more headings.

File Size — What are the upper limits on file size? This is not quite the same thing as maximum number of records. For example, you might have 2,000 records spread over two disk drives. The system can handle the total. But if you want to sort the entire file *across* disk drives, you may run into trouble. This typically is a problem only with very large applications.

Fixed Field or Variable Length Records — Fixed field means the same number of characters is always set aside for a data element, regardless of the actual size of individual entries. Thus, like data elements always occur in the same place in the record. The software searches by place, rather than by matching information. Variable length means you only use the space you need. But because the computer doesn't know where your data element begins or ends, you have to give it some additional coding to know what it's looking at. Fixed field is easier to use but wasteful of storage. Ideally, a system should be able to handle both.

Characters Matched — In list processing, you want the computer to either sort or select records from a list, depending upon the criteria you specify. The more characters the software matches in sorting or selecting, the better the accuracy. Otherwise, if you have similar names or part numbers you will have problems. Thirty characters per match is a good number.

Look-up Tables — If you are building a personnel list, for example, you might want to conserve storage by using a code for each person's job title. The look-up table, sometimes called a translation table, allows you to display or print the full title for each code when needed. The best systems allow you to create look-up tables for the fields in your records, and merge these with the records for output.

Range Tests — Some list processing software allows you to specify that a field must be alphabetical or numerical, or that it must contain so many characters. If the typist makes a mistake during entry, the machine sounds an alarm. If the machine is sophisticated, it will even let you specify a range for valid numerical entries.

Types of Searches Performed — A full Boolean search capability allows greater than, and/or equal to, and/or less than in any combination you set up.

Select Levels — How many search criteria, called qualifers, can you specify in a single pass? For instance, a school district uses list processing to keep track of substitute teachers. The administration may want to know all the substitutes who can teach high school language courses, who will accept work for five or more days at a stretch, and who are willing to travel to remote areas in the district. You should be able to specify six or more qualifiers in a single pass through the file.

Sort Levels — This refers to a sort within a sort within a sort. To go back to our example, let's sort the list by level of school taught, and within each of those categories by subject taught, and within each subject area, in order of hiring preference by seniority or length of experience. Again, you should be able to handle five or six nested levels in a single pass.

Types of Sorts — Will it sort in both ascending and descending alphabetical and numerical order? Some systems only go from A to Z, not vice versa. Watch out for restrictions. Can you sort in ascending numerical order on one level and descending alphabetical order on the second level in the same pass?

Selective Printing — How well does the system handle selective printing? Let's say that once you have completed your selection, you only want to print the names of the teachers — not their complete records. How complex is the reformatting?

Speed — How fast is the system? How long will it take to do a three-level select of a file if 50% of the records meet your criteria? How long to do a three-level sort of the entire file? There is no standard per se, since the answer varies with the size of the file. However, make sure that you can live with any limits the system imposes.

Simultaneous Operations — Can list processing be handled as a background operation? In a shared-resource system, will it draw so heavily on the central processor that other editing operations slow down or halt?

Working Storage — If you are sorting, the system most likely will maintain the master and create a copy to your new instructions. If your list is very large, you may run into storage problems. Make sure you have enough.

Special Packages — Some vendors offer packaged list processing applications, such as Executive Schedule Management. This package allows the WP typist to sort several managers' schedules, compare available time slots, and arrange a convenient meeting time. These kinds of applications are easy to set up individually, if not offered for free by the vendor.

Mathematics

Functions — Will the system add — both horizontally and vertically — subtract, multiply, and divide? Calculate percentages and negative balances? Other features?

Programming — Is it programmable — in the sense that a desk-top calculator can be programmed to remember a sequence of calculations, not in a true data processing sense? How many steps? Can you store this program?

Number Registers — How many number registers are there? If you are using your word processor as a calculator, you will want storage registers in which you can accumulate subtotals.

Today, maybe it's easier to ask what it won't do.

Glossary and UDKs (User-defined Keys)

UDK technology is merging into data processing. Some systems not only allow you to link up a sequence of commands, but also incorporate some limited decision-making, even making numeric comparisons. Based on the comparison, the program can loop (perform the same sequence again with a new variable) or it can jump to another place in the program. One vendor claims it took a Fortran programmer 13 hours to write the same report program that a WP operator developed in one hour using UDK capabilities. With this in mind, glossary and UDK evaluation criteria are as follows:

What are the restrictions? How much storage can be set aside for the glossary? Is there a minimum/maximum number of terms allowable? Is there a maximum number of characters allowed per term?

What coding structure is used to recall glossary terms? If you have a shared-resource system with several operators, do the operators share the glossary, or does each typist create an individual library?

Can you display or print the codes and the complete glossary? It does no good to create it if you can't remember what you did.

How do you set up user-definable keys? What are the capabilities and restrictions? In other words, how long and complex a procedure can you define? Can you integrate list processing and math in your stored procedures? How many UDKs can you have?

Are the UDKs a substitute for good WP software? This is, of course, a subjective question. But watch out for machines that try to accomplish standard formatting and editing features with UDKs. This option should be reserved for extras.

PERIPHERALS

In evaluating competing systems, consider each machine's overall flexibility and growth potential. Some things you may want to look for:

Mag-card Interface — Very useful if you are converting a large stock of mag cards. If you are converting from one vendor's disk to another, there are commercial services which can do this. Ask your vendor for assistance.

OCR Interface — Available?

Photocomposition Interface — Available?

Telecommunications Interface — Available? Will it talk to your computer and to TWX or telex networks?

Data Processing — Can you run computer programs other than WP?

That's the list of selection criteria. Use it wisely and it will help you pick the right equipment, as well as saving you from any rude surprises.

10

Data Processing with a Word Processor

Data processing concerns the manipulation of items of information. It involves raw data and numbers more than sentences and paragraphs. DP is used to tabulate monthly sales volume; WP is used to print and distribute the report.

More and more systems are merging these two activities to offer true information processing. Applications which are often run on WP/DP systems include accounts payable and receivable, inventory control and general ledger. Some, such as general ledger programs, are highly computational. Others, such as inventory management, are close cousins to list processing.

HOW TO DEVELOP THE SYSTEM

In order to run DP programs on a WP system, you need a means of translating your written instructions — or programs — into a language the machine understands. This is provided by the vendor as a compiler, or programming language. The most common are BASIC, COBOL and FORTRAN.

The compiled machine language is executed by an operating system. There are a number of choices — CP/M is used for many microprocessors because it works well with many software packages. As a user, you have little choice in how your system is set up. But it is useful to learn about operating systems, as some are more efficient than others. The publications list at the back of the book lists some resources for additional information.

The text-editing software in your WP system is a program. It was written by the vendor in a programming language — possibly BASIC. This is an easy language for people to work with because it uses English terms such as READ, PRINT, END, etc. When all the WP program instructions are written, they are keyboarded into the system and interpreted into machine language. This means that the BASIC instruction for PRINT is translated into a code the microprocessor can act on.

Once this is done, the vendor can store the machine language code on a program diskette. This is what you load into your machine each day to make it a word processor. The vendor does not need to include compiling capability — the ability to translate more BASIC programs into machine language — on the system sitting in your office. Without it, your machine is strictly a word processor. If, however, the vendor sells a BASIC or other compiler with the system, then you can use it to load as many additional programs as you wish — subject to the limitations of the hardware.

A Sample Program

By way of explanation, we will start with the example of a very simple program to keep track of expense accounts. We want to add up each employee's expenses, distribute them according to client and type of expense, compare actual against budgeted expenses, and then come up with grand totals for all departments and the company as a whole.

The first thing we want to do is enter each employee's name and list of expenses, followed by the codes that identify the client and the kind of expense (travel, entertainment and so forth). Using WP we can keyboard all the data into the system. But how do we tell the computer to do the rest?

We need to be able to write instructions, or a program, saying: "Recognize each item of information for what it is, tabulate expenditures according to the various categories, and produce a report." This is what a BASIC or other compiler in your system is all about. It is very different from having list or math processing as part of your WP software — because you can now control what the computer is able to do.

A Word of Warning

The worst mistake you can make is to assume that because an office system offers both WP and DP, it will satisfy both sets of needs. More people buy the wrong machine for the job, particularly when they get into data processing, than would care to admit it.

Office users who are considering information processing often look at word processing systems first. The equipment is presented as a complete package, and is described in understandable office terminology. The unfamiliar world of computers, by contrast, can be overwhelming. However, many dual purpose systems do not offer equally good WP and DP. Even if they do, this is no guarantee that the WP and DP are equally suited to your needs. Caution is recommended, or you are likely to end up with a lopsided system that satisfies no one.

HOW TO AVOID THE PITFALL

First and foremost, analyze your WP and DP needs separately and thoroughly. The first chapters of this book explain in detail how to do this for WP. How, you ask, are we going to deal with the whole of DP in a single chapter? By establishing some simple ground rules.

First, the basic analysis is straightforward. You need to describe the information in quantitative and qualitative terms, telling what it is and what you want to do with it.

Second, we will confine our discussion to information systems that are local and involve common office records. By local, I mean systems dedicated to a specific work group or office function. If you need to design an engineering-oriented system for a corporation of 500 persons, this is neither the right book nor the appropriate level of technology. We will concentrate on routine daily tasks, such as pulling information from files or billing clients in a law firm.

Third, when the type of analysis or type of equipment discussed in this book does not fit your problem, you will need to expand your search to other technologies, such as large-scale computer systems.

Fourth, underlying all of the above is an assumption that you need word processing in the first place. If not, then rule three applies.

CATEGORIES OF WP/DP SYSTEMS

In the following sections we will discuss the art of translating your information problems into data processing terms. However, before delving too far into analysis, we need to examine the systems choices you will have at the end of your work. Basically the categories include: DP systems which offer WP as an option; WP systems equipped with standard programs; WP systems equipped with custom programs; personal computers; and professional workstations.

DP Systems

True data processing systems have always had some kind of text-editing capability. This evolved as a means of revising data and cleaning up programs; the emphasis is on editing functions rather than on formatting. Thus, these programs do not offer margin justification, half-spacing, decimal tab alignment and the like. Because these early text editors were designed for DP professionals, they are complicated to use and require a lot of coding and memorization. Today, this bias is gradually disappearing. However, as a *general* rule, data processing systems are better at DP than WP.

WP Systems

If you start looking at systems oriented toward WP, the reverse of the rule applies. Word processors *tend* to be better at WP than DP. For instance, they are slower when it comes to processing large transaction files. This makes them poor candidates for handling thousands of records. They also are limited to doing one or two operations at a time; a heavy DP application might slow down or stop text-editing operations completely. Again, this bias is gradually disappearing. But it is worth keeping in mind.

If you select a word processor with DP capability you have two ways to go: either buy standard programs developed for the general market or develop your own. There are many excellent general applications programs on the market. If you can find a close match, the general program will cost you about 20% of what a custom program will run. The trick is to find a close match.

Custom programs are written specifically for your operation. You do not have to modify your methods in any way. However, they are much more expensive, particularly if you do not have in-house programming services. You will also find them quite expensive in terms of your own time. You will have to work quite closely with systems analysts and programmers to make sure they understand what you want. This is essential to ensure that the programs meet your needs.

A reasonable alternative is to buy a general software package (or set of programs) and modify it to your needs. Instead of reinventing the wheel, you will spend your money improving its efficiency. Either the developer of the software package — who may or may not be the WP vendor — or a programmer of your choosing can make the modifications for you. Either way, get all agreements in writing, including cost estimates.

In order to make modifications to a standard software package, you will need sufficient documentation — usually source and object code — so that your programmer can understand the setup and make the necessary changes. Most likely, the vendor of the standard software will ask you not to sell the program or its modifications in any way. This is common procedure to protect copyrighted material.

If you have custom programs developed, be sure to clarify who owns them. If the programmer (or software house, as this service is called) retains ownership, you should get a significant break on the development cost. The software house does this because they want to sell your software to more customers. Make sure you have some say in whether it is sold to your competition.

Personal Computers

Personal computers are really a subset of DP systems. They were designed to be cheap enough to be within the range of the home hobby user. However, they have carved a real niche for themselves in business as well. The term personal computer is apt, because these systems tend to be dedicated to a single user or a very limited set of functions. There is a wide variety of systems available, and most offer a wide variety of programs developed by independent sources. These include word processing and graphics programs.

Personal computers are mentioned here because so many users are turning to them for low cost word processing. Typically these systems sacrifice convenience and vendor support for low price and the ability to run more programs.

One of the ways in which personal computers trade convenience for economy is by using general purpose terminals that lack the special function keys found on most word processors. It frequently takes several keystrokes to execute a single command, because each key must serve so many purposes. Likewise, the programs are not as rich in functions as those on dedicated word processors. Proportional spacing, for example, is not usually offered. Thus, personal computers are not as easy to use, nor do they offer the quality some businesses need.

Personal computer vendors do not usually offer MSR support. These systems are often bought through retail outlets, many of which understand the needs of the hobbyist better than those of the business user. Maintenance contracts may or may not be available. Often, users even have to find their own sources for programs.

Why, then, the great interest in personal computers? First of all, because of their relatively low price. Second, because these systems do offer pre-packaged computer software, and some of it is quite good. Programs for financial management, forecasting, and even business graphics are very attractive. You can set up and manipulate your own information files without having to depend on a central data processing service.

The potential volume of the personal computer market has been recognized by the major WP/DP systems vendors. They are beginning to offer competitive systems with many of the rough edges mentioned above shaved off. Furthermore, they are offering the resources to link personal computers into office systems that provide individual independence but still permit the sharing of text, data and peripheral devices such as printers. If you are planning to set up multifunction systems in your office, be sure to investigate the possibilities of personal computers before deciding on more expensive systems.

Professional Workstations

Professional workstations are just beginning to arrive on the market. These systems also offer word and data processing, usually of very high quality. They are also designed to be very easy to use. No prior data processing expertise is required.

Professional workstations offer the ability to compose and edit text, create business graphics such as bar charts and simple diagrams, perform extended calculator functions, and file and retrieve information. For example, you can develop presentation documents, incorporating multiple typestyles on a single page, as well as sophisticated pie charts showing various alternatives. The system will not only compute all the alternatives, but will graph them out as well. When a series of professional workstations are linked together, as they are designed to be, they can also be used to send and receive messages, text and data.

To some extent professional workstations can be viewed as top-of-the-line personal computers. They combine in a single-vendor package the best of the programs that people are trying to put together on their personal machines. Professional workstations are ideally suited to knowledge workers, the people who develop and present ideas and projects. They are less the tool of top management than of middle managers and professional staff. Professional workstations perform the functions of a top-flight administrative assistant with some specialized data manipulation and graphics skills.

At present, professional workstations are priced at the very high end of the word processing market. The vendors have targeted large corporations as their principal market, and only make the price attractive through quantity discounts. Thus, these systems are out of range for most small businesses. However, it is the small business owner who is most likely to be undersupported and to need the convenient range of services that a professional workstation provides.

Sooner or later, low cost professional workstations will be available. If you are planning to use a system yourself, or if you are planning to assign it to a professional rather than to a typist, be sure to investigate the possibility of using a computer specifically designed as a professional workstation.

How to Choose

If you plan to run programs on a WP/DP system, you can save yourself some time by looking for software packages first and systems second. Another one of those general rules: it is harder to find good software than good hardware.

If, for example, a law firm wants to automate both its typing and its client billing, the latter will be the more difficult task. If the firm finds an acceptable client billing package, the WP will likely be acceptable as well. However, if the billing program is not good, the quality of WP won't matter.

Finally, don't forget that there are many excellent computer service bureaus. If you are not sure about DP, using the resources of a commercial service is a good way to start out. With a minimum investment of time and money, you can evaluate the benefits of DP for your operation. When you are ready, you can move the operation in-house. However, unless you are very lucky, the service bureau program cannot be made to run on your own computer. The money spent on the service bureau will not apply to the cost of your own system, nor will it spare you a second complete conversion of your records.

THE SYSTEMS ANALYSIS

The purpose of a systems analysis is to translate your understanding of your problem into terms a systems vendor or programmer can understand. It has two objectives. First, your analysis will help you to match your requirements with standard program offerings, since both will be expressed in similar terms. Second, your analysis will help determine the hardware capacity — expressed in terms of the size of the computer and its data storage — which you will need to handle all your programs, including WP.

A good systems analysis has one other function: cleaning up your manual operation. Remember our hypothetical expense account program at the beginning of this chapter? If the problem is simply one of excessive manual posting and duplicate record keeping, the computer can help. But if the underlying problem is the collection of inaccurate or incomplete information, the computer reports won't be any better than the manual ones. Make sure the operation you plan to computerize functions manually before you add automation.

Files and Records

The initial focus of your analysis is on the information in your files. WP deals with documents. If you have a large collection of related documents, much as you would in a cabinet, you think of them as a file. In DP, we talk about records, again collected in files. These are the building blocks of programs. A list processing application, such as the substitute teacher's roster we talked about earlier, is a small-scale example of a file. Each teacher is a record; the entire set is the file. In DP systems the principle is the same, although the files are often more complex.

Data Bases and Structured Programs

A more sophisticated way of looking at computer files is something called a data base. In concept, it is much like list processing but on a larger scale. You collect sets of information about specific customers, products, or whatever. The same categories of information are collected for each, building a file of records.

DBMS Software

Using special software, called a data base management system (DBMS), the information in the records can be processed and reported in almost unlimited ways. It differs from traditional data processing in that the same information may be used in several programs for a variety of purposes. In other words, instead of creating a set of specific reports on a computer, you create a file of information common to many reports. This information is then selectively formatted and output to meet individual document requirements.

DBMS software allows you to formulate quesitons and manipulate the information in the system. This is how reports are generated. However, because the system gives you so much ability to tailor your information requests, many routine reports can be eliminated. For example, instead of traditional monthly reports of all sales, you can concentrate on those with exceptionally low volume one month, and those in a new territory the next.

Properly used, these data base packages can greatly enhance your access to filed information. In a paper file, your access is limited to the ways in which you can physically segregate the paper: by cabinet, drawer and folder — let's say, by year, category of customer and then alphabetically by customer name.

If you want to keep track of the same folder two ways — say by name and number — you need a cross-index. If you want to research a special question, such as how many new customers make large purchases, the clerical effort may be more costly than it's worth. A computer, however, can keep track of all the index terms — year, type of customer, name, number — and handle all the special items, too.

DBMS applications can be costly. Not only do you need hardware, but you have to enter all that information in the system. The clerical time required to key in the data is a significant part of the total cost. Unless you can eliminate repetitive keyboarding of the same information for several reports, the expense is difficult to justify.

Choosing the Right Applications

When you design your DP system, you will need to focus your thinking on how you want to structure your files. Data base systems are very useful when you have a large set of information to output in a variety of routine and special reports. However, because data bases are so flexible, they require more constant management attention — they are not very good at handling automatic reporting cycles or computational programs.

General ledger accounting and accounts receivable are examples of applications better handled as traditional programs. Report formats are highly structured. The emphasis is on process — the routine calculations which are performed on the data once it is entered in the system. The outputs — such as a balance sheet or an invoice — are also highly standardized. In this case, flexibility is traded for the convenience of a fully automated procedure.

Many systems offer some ability to merge data base and structured programming capability. An accounts receivable file, for instance, can be used to provide special management information, as well as to compute monthly invoices. It is important to master the difference between these two concepts early in your systems analysis, and to apply each to your best advantage.

SYSTEMS DESIGN

The next step, then, is to set up your files. Whether they are part of a data base or a structured program, you'll need to describe the following: How many records per file? How long is each record? What fields (or data elements) must each contain? Are the fields fixed or variable length?

Will information be coded to save space? For instance, a substitute teacher qualified to teach high school might be coded H, for "high school." A customer file is likely to be coded by number, since straight name files are harder to sort.

Will the code interpretations be controlled manually, or will the computer keep track of this information in look-up tables? In other words, if you code your customer files by number, how will you keep track of which number goes with which name?

How often will the information be input? Updated? Searched online? Reported out?

How long will records remain current? How many new records will be added during that time? Do you turn your records over each year, or do you keep most of them and add some new ones. Try to predict your maximum storage requirements over the life of the system — usually five years.

What is the purpose of the file? How does it relate to other files in the system? For example, a sales transaction might generate an invoice, an inventory update, a backorder for out-of-stock items and a sales commission. Each of these represents a different but related file: accounts payable, inventory control, stock ordering and sales commission payments.

What information processing do you want to perform? You might want the system to prepare a complete invoice, including computation of unit and extended prices, local and state taxes, discounts and total amounts due. Describe the purpose and major functions of your system.

What will the outputs look like? Will there be standard forms and reports? How does the output information link up with the files in your system?

Who will the users of the system be? Will they have direct, online access, or will they receive printed reports? Who will input information and who will be in charge of output? How does information get into the system in the first place?

What are you willing to pay? This gets back to that old question of justifying the cost of the system. Most likely, you will find your new system costs you something out of pocket. But it may open up new and profitable ways of doing business. As with WP, you should have a firm idea of what your criteria for cost-benefits will be before you go too deeply into your systems analysis.

By thinking through these and other questions, you can describe your data processing application in concrete terms. If possible, make a flow chart of a complete information cycle from data collection through processing and deletion of expired records. The discipline of a flow chart will ensure that there are no gaps in the logic of your design.

WRITING A PROGRAM SPECIFICATION

The outcome of the analysis is a program specification. It is your statement of what the system is to contain and how it must perform. It should be outlined in terms that suppliers of software packages can respond to.

Software houses will use your specification to demonstrate what they can and cannot do. Developers of custom software will use it as the model from which to develop your own programs.

Two sample program specifications are given here, to use as models in developing your own. The first specification is for a data base system. In this example, we are really outlining performance requirements: how much data storage, processed how fast, in what general ways. The vendor really has no need to know what the data elements are or what the reports must contain. All we are looking for is a system of sufficient power and flexibility.

The second specification involves a traditional, structured program. The specification defines the broad parameters of the system: file contents, kinds of transactions and kinds of outputs.

Software houses propose various packages which fall within the stated parameters. In a sense, it is like providing an outline with the vendors filling in the detail. If you choose to have custom programs written, you can plan on working with analysts and programmers to fill in all of the detail yourself.

Case #1: Apprentice Training Program

This data base is used to manage a government-coordinated apprenticeship and training program. By law, the state enrolls and monitors the progress of all apprentices in trade union training programs. At any given time, there are about 6,000 enrollees plus 3,000 new applicants. Each enrollee stays in the program an average of four years.

During the training time, there are countless letters and other documents involving the apprentice, the union and any of 33 apprenticeship and training committees. Likewise, there are federal and other mandated reports. These tabulate the participation in the program according to race, sex, age, trade and so forth.

From Manual to Computerized System

In a manual system, each apprentice's record consists of an index card; an eight-foot file holds all the cards. Misfiles are common. Names, addresses and other information are copied from the cards countless times. It takes almost two months of manual counting and typing to compile the quarterly statistics and reports. With that much lag, a current report is never available.

Clearly, this application is a candidate for computerization. The fact that so much of the information is output as letters and reports makes it a good candidate for a WP/DP system. The secretaries refer constantly to the file cards in their preparation of routine documents.

An analysis of the document cycle establishes the data elements to be carried in each applicant's and enrollee's record. The analysis concentrates on the items that are used repetitively in WP applications and that are tabulated for regular and special reports. A specification is written for the software. In addition, the vendors are asked to provide detailed information about the hardware they propose to use.

Specification Components

The software specification looks like this, with some extra explanatory material added for your information:

- Maintain a data base of 10,000 800-character records, divided into 100 variable length fields. Of the 100 fields, 25 are key fields. The rest may be printed, but will not be used for sorting the file or matching selection criteria. Key fields are identified and retrieved by a two-character code.

- System to display screens to guide operator during input and editing. A "screen" is similar to a forms facsimile. It prompts the typist through each data element in the order of occurrence in the record. When a typist enters a new record, working with a structured screen is more efficient than staring at a blank display.

- System to check for logic of entries on a field-by-field basis. If any entry requires a code of M or F for sex, the system will reject an entry of G. This is a kind of automatic proofreading. This kind of software is sophisticated and not always available on small systems.

- System to display or print complete record, short-form summary record, or selected fields as requested by operator. For simplicity's sake, you do not want to look at the entire record when all you are interested in is the name and address.

- System to generate standard reports automatically, as well as one-time reports on command. Automatic report generation is beyond the capability of most list processing software; this requires DP.

- System to perform all records selection and sort operations specified below, without regard for the capacity of individual disk drives.

- Sort in ascending or descending alphabetical or numerical order. Sort up to six levels in single pass.

- Sort entire file at a rate of at least four records per second, with concurrent text-editing operations. Note that this means about 50 minutes for the entire file. In this case, the sorting speed is not a problem. However, it is relatively slow in DP terms.

- Select records on the basis of greater than, and/or equal to, and/or less than. Match up to six selections per pass.

- Select records at the rate of 20 records per second. Match up to 30 characters in sorting or selecting records.

- Display number of records meeting search criteria. Sometimes you just want to know how many, rather than who. After performing a select, therefore, all you really want to know is how many records fit the search criteria.

- WP/DP operations to be fully integrated (transparent).

Case #2: Law Firm

The second specification was developed to identify automated client accounting software for a law firm. The requirements include tracking different types of billing activities and tabulating these in monthly statements. In addition, the firm wants to use the information collected in the billing process to monitor individual productivity.

Most charges to clients are assessed on the basis of time spent multiplied by the attorney's billing rate. This is usually accounted for in tenths of hours. An attorney over the course of a month may generate dozens of time reports for a single client. When there are several attorneys and several hundred clients, sorting and posting these time reports to the correct account becomes a monumental task.

Certain standard services, such as preparing wills, are performed on a fixed-fee basis. However, the firm still wants to keep track of the time involved in order to know if the flat rates are adequate.

In addition, the firm advances costs to clients for copying, court filing fees, etc. These must be accounted for and billed. Finally, the firm accepts retainer payments and manages trust accounts. The payment disbursements, and balances of these accounts must be included in client statements.

Prior to being sent to the client, each statement is reviewed by a partner in the firm. Sometimes the bill is adjusted for one reason or another. For instance, a junior attorney may have worked six hours on a matter, which the managing partner believes is too long. The charge to the client will be reduced.

In some cases, the attorney may wish to provide a detailed statement for each activity billed. For example, a conference to review a lease or discuss the preliminary draft of a will might be cited. In other cases, a summary will do.

With regard to management reporting, the partners want to assess how well each attorney performs. What percent of the total hours worked was Attorney A's? What percent of the total receipts was Attorney A's? These should, of course, be in balance. The firm also wants to monitor productivity by type of case. What percent of the total hours worked was spent on wills? What percent of the total receipts came from wills? If there is an imbalance, the firm's management will want to react.

Request for Proposals

With all this in mind, a request for proposals was developed. The first part is a cover letter describing the firm and its needs. This provides a frame of reference. It also gives an indication of the types of programs and numbers of records that will be involved. The second part deals with the specific capabilities of the program.

The part of the cover letter describing the organization and general requirements is summarized like this:

> The law firm of Mirco and Bruce plans to automate its client accounting. The firm has six attorneys, plus five paralegals and assistants whose time is billed for some activities. The firm opens about 1,200 new cases per year and maintains about 600 continuing cases. Case load is growing about 10% a year.
>
> There are 250 time/activity reports per day, all posted to client ledger cards. In addition, there are about 750 fee postings to ledgers each month. These consist of fee filings, advanced costs — such as travel — and miscellaneous expenses.
>
> Each month, 600 statements are issued. About half are first-time statements. The rest are for past due accounts. A total of 250 receipts is posted to the ledger during the billing cycle.
>
> Mirco and Bruce is in general practice. The firm handles 25 categories of law, including domestic relations, personal injury, real estate and business organization. Depending on the attorney or paralegal involved, there are three different billing rates in use. Fixed fees are charged for 15 specific types of actions, such as wills, uncontested divorces and so forth. There are also 10 categories of unbillable time, such as administraton, which must be reported. All attorney and paralegal time must be accounted for by type of activity, regardless of whether it is billable.

Program Specification

Figure 10.1 is a flow chart of the proposed system necessary for an overview, and the detailed program specification. Note the logical progression from input records to output records and reports. Using the information supplied in the letter above, try to compute the total size of the system this firm will require by filling in the appropriate number of client records in the example below. You will have to devise your own estimate of how many characters are appropriate for the various fields of information.

WRAPPING IT UP

When you are evaluating packages, the most important criteria are the suitability of the programs, the quality of the system (hardware and support), and the cost. There are, however, some less obvious questions that you should also ask:

Additional Questions

Are WP and DP operations fully integrated on the system (transparent)? Remember, many dual-function systems run WP and DP as mutually exclusive activities.

Is multi-programming accommodated? Even if WP and DP operations are transparent to each other, the system may not be powerful enough to handle full-scale WP and DP operations simultaneously. Or, if you have several DP programs, the same restriction may apply. Make sure you understand all the limits of your system.

Is the system fast enough? Try to get an estimate of how long it will take to complete a cycle, such as sorting the entire file, producing a complete set of monthly statements, or whatever. Processing speeds can vary by a factor of 10 or more. If you have to wait two hours every time you want to rearrange your data, you may be looking at the wrong system.

How good is the program documentation? Sooner or later, you will want to change the program. The vendor who sold it to you may be long gone. Good documentation means that a qualified programmer can pick up where the original developer left off. If the supplier won't share complete access to the documentation, make sure you pick one with good prospects for survival.

How good is the support? Will you and your staff receive adequate training?

(Text continues on page 146)

Figure 10.1 Flow Chart of System

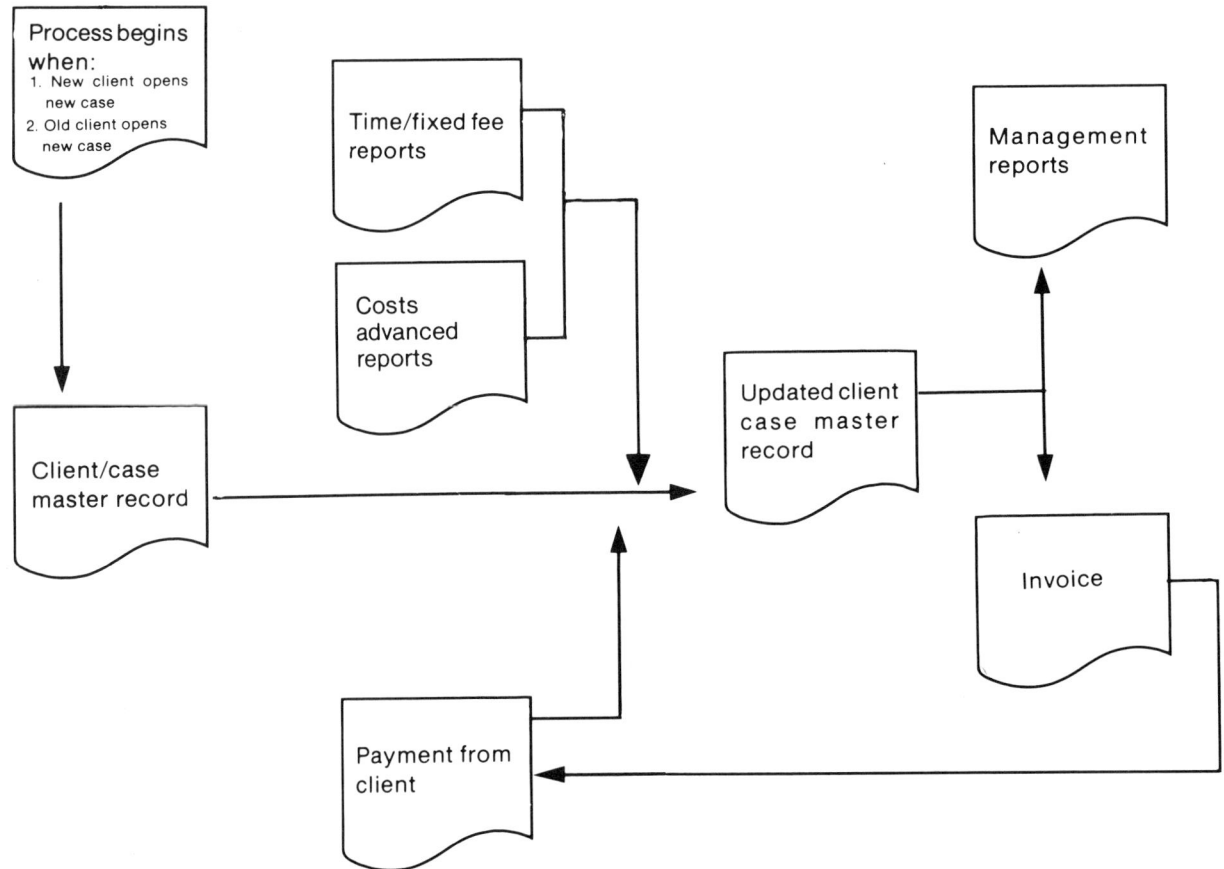

Figure 10.1 Flow Chart of System continued

I. Input Records

    A. Online Records — These are the records that will be stored on magnetic media. They must be described in terms of their contents (a list of the information they contain) and their size (number of characters).

       Client Master Record File — Each client has one record; the entire set of records is a file.

        1. Record contents

           (a) Client information — one occurrence per record

               client name/spouse name
               home address and phone
               work address and phone

           (b) Case information — up to four cases per client record

               type case
               responsible member of firm
               date opened
               date closed
               amount billed — date last bill
               amount paid — date last payment
               amount due

           (c) Billing entry information — up to 40 entries per case

               person's initials (member of firm i.d.)
               time spent (in 1/10th hours)
               type of activity (if fixed fee)
               narrative of entry (up to 200 characters)

           (d) Costs advanced information — up to 40 entries per case

               type of cost
               amount

        2. File Size — This should be projected for the first year and for the next five years — the expected life of the system. In addition to being an important component of a program design, the file size is used to determine the amount of diskette or disk storage the system must have. Remember to allow enough storage for your data files, WP files, program files, and work space. If you want to sort a 1MB alpha file into numeric order, you will need an additional 1MB (two in all) for working storage.

Figure 10.1 Flow Chart of System continued

      (a)   Total number of records — number of active clients, now and in five years.

      (b)   Maximum number characters per record — This is computed by determining the number of characters in each field (or data element), and then adding all the characters in all the fields together. This is the amount of storage that must be allowed for each record.

      (c)   Total file size — the number of records and the number of characters each.

B. Offline Records — These are records that are used to create and update the master records. They contain information that is keyed into the master file, but they are not stored on computer per se. Because they are source documents, it is important that their contents and format meet your needs.

   1. Time/Fixed Fee Activity Report

      case name/number
      person's initials (member of firm i.d.)
      time spent
      type of activity (if fixed fee)
      narrative of activity

   2. Costs Advanced Report

      case name/number
      type of cost
      amount

   3. Payment Received

      case name/number
      amount received
      date of payment

II. Output Records

   A.   Invoice — Format and Contents

      client name and address
      case name and number
      list of month's billing entries

          attorney   narrative description of   amount
                           type of fixed fee activity

      list of month's costs advanced
                type of cost   amount

Figure 10.1 Flow Chart of System continued

        total new charges
        previous balance
        payments received
        current amount due

    B.   Management Reports — Format and Contents

        number of hours worked: by each type of case and for all cases

        amount billed: by each type of case and for all cases

        number of billable and non-billable hours worked: by each attorney and for all attorneys

        amount billed: by each attorney

        number of hours worked: by type of fixed fee and all fixed fee charges

        amount billed: by type of fixed fee and for all fixed fee charges

        number of cases open, number new cases, number cases closed

        total amount new charges, total amount previously due, total amount payments received, current outstanding balance

III.   Qualitative Summary of System

    Number of:

        clients
        types of cases — and coding structure
        professionals (whose time will be tracked)
        types of fixed fees — and coding structure
        types of costs advanced — and coding structure

    Number of:

        open cases — average workload
        time/fixed fee reports per day/month
        costs advanced reports per day/month
        invoices prepared/month
        payments posted/month

    Run cycle for management reports (daily? monthly?)

    Number of hours per month to update records, produce invoices and management reports? (In other words, what are your time requirements?)

If the vendor improves the package, will you receive these updates? Will someone be available to answer questions and assist you with conversion?

Has anyone else used this program successfully? References, references, references.

Your Responsibilities

No matter how good the system is, you will have some responsibilities as well. For any kind of complex system with multi-terminals and/or multi-programs, you should put someone with systems experience in charge.

You or your systems manager will need to establish procedures to ensure that data is entered correctly. Key entries must be proofread (or verified, in DP language). Your data files also require backup, so that they are not lost in the event of a disaster or systems failure. This means a regular procedure to duplicate diskettes or disks and transfer them to security storage.

Your systems manager should also be responsible for evaluating the performance of the system. If it is underutilized, or if its capacity is inadequate at some point, you must be alerted in time to react. Like any system, whether it be manual, WP or DP, its value increases in direct proportion to its managers' and users' involvement and expertise.

11
Optical Character Readers

Optical character readers, also called OCR or optical scanners, read typed text and record the information they see on magnetic media. Typically, this is a diskette. Editing can then be done on the word processor, even though the keyboarding was done on a standard electric typewriter. Sound appealing? Read on.

WHY OCR?

OCR expands the input and the output network of a word processing system. It makes any typewriter an input station. Somewhere between 40% and 70% of most word processing is keyboarding: getting the information stored on the system. Using OCR, you can do this on a $1,000 typewriter, instead of a $12,000 word processor. (See Figure 11.1.) For straight inputting — as opposed to formatting and editing — there is no real advantage to using a WP typewriter.

Figure 11.1 Diagram of OCR Process

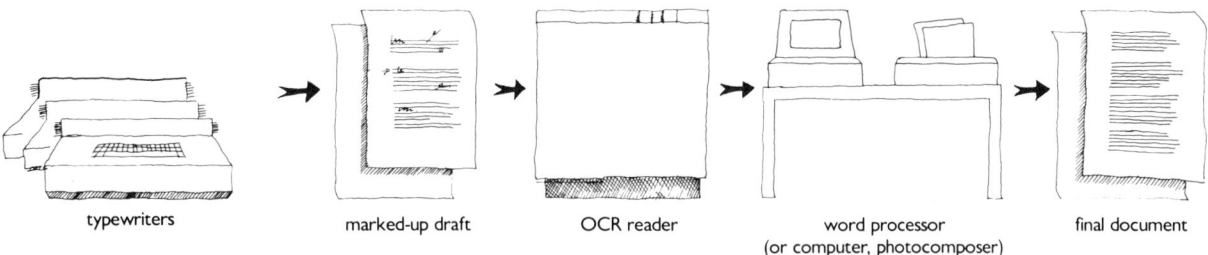

typewriters → marked-up draft → OCR reader → word processor (or computer, photocomposer) → final document

The same rationale, of course, applies to data processing. Data entry typically accounts for 10% to 25% of a DP budget. OCR reduces the need for expensive data entry equipment. Decentralizing input to the originators ensures that the people most likely to spot problems enter the information.

One OCR reader can handle the input of up to 40 secretaries. A fast machine can read several hundred pages an hour. OCR is used to give occasional or remote users access to WP. It also is an excellent way to handle peaks. You don't have to buy more equipment than you need for everyday applications. OCR can soften the impact of a reorganization that might otherwise be necessary to justify word processing.

OCR also expands the output network of the total system. A single reader can communicate with several different word processors (although not simultaneously), as well as with TWX and Telex telegraphic networks, photocomposers, computers and remote data terminals. This interface flexibility is the key to OCR's future.

Finally, OCR can be used for WP media conversion. The documents stored on one machine's diskette can be printed out and read onto a second machine's diskette. The format does not always transfer perfectly (see below), but it is a lot faster than re-keyboarding.

WHY NOT OCR?

Two reasons: cost and reliability. To date, the cost of readers has not decreased at the same rate as for word processors. Thus, you must have a requirement for three or four workstations before OCR becomes cost-effective. With electronic typewriters and other low-scale equipment on the market, OCR is not necessarily the cheapest way to equip occasional users.

Reliability is a big problem. Readers make two kinds of errors: "can't reads" and "misreads." The former are no problem. The machine does not recognize a character and alerts the operator. (It may simply stop until the correct character is keyed in, or it may display a blinking asterisk to indicate a problem.) Either way, the operator is in control. Up to five "can't reads" per page is considered acceptable.

Misreads range from one character in every 10,000 characters (five pages) to one in every 100,000 (50 pages). Two things affect reliability: the typeface used and the cost of the machine. As a general rule, stylized typefaces are easier for the machine to read. And, the more expensive the machine, the better its track record tends to be. To understand the relationship of typefaces and reliability, let's take a closer look at the equipment.

HOW OCR WORKS

There are four components to a scanner: the paper transport, the scanning mechanism, recognition logic and post-recognition logic. In addition, many machines have a keyboard and display, as well as a window so that you can look at the line being scanned. (See Figure 11.2.)

Paper Transport

The paper transport moves paper to the scanning mechanism and then deposits it in output bins. It is this technology that keeps the cost of scanners so high. Transports account for 50% of the cost and 80% of the problems.

Scanning Mechanism

The scanning mechanism reduces the images on a page to black and white patterns. The degree of contrast between text and background and the reflectivity of the paper affect the efficiency of the mechanism: the more contrast and reflectivity the better. (In other words, don't use earth-toned, deckle-finished letterhead.)

Recognition Logic

Recognition logic translates patterns seen by the scanner into digital information. This process is dependent upon recognizing pattern boundaries, such as the beginning and end of a character and the beginning and end of a line. The pattern seen by the scanner is compared with a character matrix stored in the system. Each typeface has its own matrix. The more expensive the machine, the more typefaces it will read.

Post-Recognition Logic

Post-recognition logic translates format and other non-character information from the page. Thus, a typist can use special marks to indicate that certain text is to be inserted or deleted, that a section of the page used for a drawing is not to be read, or that a "can't read" is to be changed to an "A." Post-recognition logic can also be used to convert WP text to input for a photo-composer (see chapter 12).

TYPEFACES

The first typeface invented for OCR was called, not too imaginatively, OCR-A. It is similar to the encoded numbers on your checks. Machines love it, because each character is uniquely distinguishable. The differences are so exaggerated that even a chipped, smudged letter pattern can still be read. However, people find OCR-A rather unattractive to work with.

Figure 11.2 OCR Reader

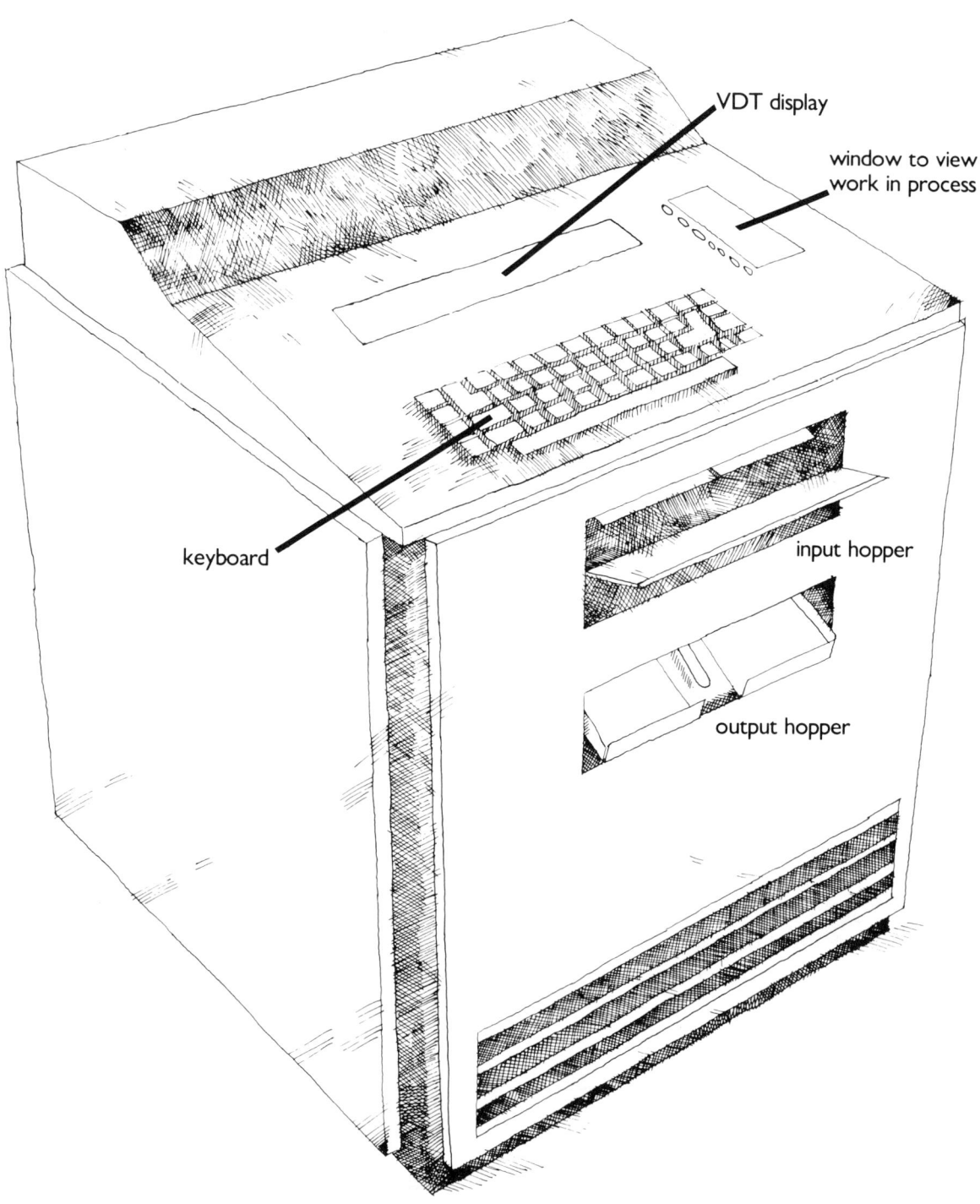

Which brings us to the next entry in the field: OCR-B. (No prizes for imagination.) It is still exaggerated enough to be acceptable to the machine. But people can live with it. However, no one would voluntarily choose it. It is only used for drafts when you know that an editing cycle will be involved.

Typefaces that offices typically use — letter gothic, prestige elite — give OCR readers fits. (Mention proportional spacing to an OCR reader and it will probably blow a fuse.) Nevertheless, there are machines that read these standard typefaces fairly well. The more you pay (typically twice or more what a word processor costs), the more flexibility and reliability you get. It is also worth noting that this technology is improving rapidly.

EVALUATION CRITERIA

Had this book been written two years ago, it would not have included a section on evaluating OCR readers. They weren't worth the trouble. They imposed rigid procedures on authors and typists, but did not produce quality output. Today, they are still trouble, but the benefits are more tangible.

If you are seriously considering OCR, you should inform yourself fully about the limitations of different vendors' equipment. Typists may have to adhere to strict procedures. Authors usually have to mark drafts in a precise way: e.g., blue pencil only, no strikeovers or erasures. Otherwise, the reader rejects the page. Graphics, letterhead and colored or textured paper can cause problems, too.

The following evaluation criteria, in addition to the points above, should help you select a suitable machine.

Input Factors

Typefaces — Which typefaces are read? How are they changed, if more than one? How many can be added?

Pitch — Can the reader handle variable pitch on a single page? Most common is 10-pitch, although 12-pitch is read on more expensive machines. Some machines read a 12-pitch font typed at 10 characters per inch — or 10-pitch. This is not the same thing as reading 12-pitch.

Interline Spacing Requirements — Can it handle single, space-and-a-half and double? Mixed on the same page? What about triple?

Subscript and Superscript Read; Underlining — An underline is less than a line space, hence the problem.

Skew Tolerances — If the lines aren't straight, the recognition logic can't define pattern boundaries. The higher the tolerance the better. For example, 1/6-inch skew tolerance over seven inches is better than 1/10-inch over the same length.

Maximum Line Length — How many characters per line? What side margins are required?

Maximum Paper Length — Top and bottom margin requirements? Smaller than letter and legal paper handled? Will it read text entered the long way on the 11-inch direction? Will the reader handle pastels, rag bond and watermarks?

Paper Weights — Most use 16-to-24-pound bond. Carbons or mixed weights cause problems.

Typewriter and Ribbon Requirements — You must generally use an unblemished typing element and a single-strike carbon ribbon to prepare input.

Blank Spaces Read — Tabs and indents may be counted incorrectly, requiring reformatting at the word processor. Blank lines sometimes result in the rest of the page being skipped.

Feeder Capabilities — How many pages stacked? From 20 to 200 is the usual range.

Editing/Processing

Error Rate — This is critical. It may vary from typeface to typeface. Ask about the frequency of both kinds of errors.

Speed in Pages per Hour — This will vary with the font, density of text, amount of formatting and so forth. Test it.

Pre-OCR Editing Procedures — Can the operator type codes that tell the machine to insert or delete characters or blocks of text? How long can the insertions be? What other special marks can be used to instruct the reader to perform a special function?

Set-up Procedures — How do you tell the machine which typeface, what line spacing, which output device?

Online Editing — If the machine can't read a character, can the operator enter the correction directly? Usually, this means some kind of display and some keyboard. The better machines give the operator the option of making corrections during scanning or during WP editing, whichever is preferred.

Forms Control Capability — This allows you to tell the machine which parts of the page to read. It gets around letterhead, graphics, signatures. Look for maximum flexibility in defining "no read" areas, and restructuring the order in which text is read.

Code-conversion — Is it user-defined? This gets into sophisticated applications, such as scientific or foreign language typing. You can expand the character set of your typewriter to incorporate the extra characters permitted on your word processor. For example, a letter with a slash through it could indicate a particular Greek letter. Who defines the codes and how they are used will be of great interest if you do this type of work.

Output Considerations

How is the reader linked to the word processor? There are three options. The first is to hard-wire the reader directly to the other machine. This is the simplest in terms of technology, but it more or less dedicates one word processor to OCR editing.

The next option is to use a telecommunications link over telephone lines. This offers more flexibility — you have access to more word processors — but the interconnect equipment is expensive.

Finally, some OCR readers output a diskette which can be read by a word processor.

More questions to ask:

If hard-wired, is input in foreground or background? If the scanner is reading to a diskette, does it tie up the display of the word processor at the same time?

How many links? Some machines have multiple "ports" or communications outlets. You can go to several word processors, to a computer, or whatever.

If not hard-wired, what media does the reader create? Although most machines output a diskette, others use paper tape or even computer tape.

How many output bins? Some readers separate out those pages with reading problems, putting them in a separate hopper.

Hardware Options

The more sophisticated machines also offer some extra options.

Displays — Anywhere from a single line to a page, these are useful for online corrections and verification. They will display the line being scanned.

Keyboards or Header Sheets — Keyboards are useful for online corrections, and also for instructing the machine in functions such as typeface or paper size to be read. Some machines use prepared "header sheets" to perform this function. The first piece of paper that goes through the transport is the instruction sheet. The machine scans the information and sets itself up accordingly.

If you plan to use OCR, start cautiously. Look for trial rentals. Give the machine a good workout. Make sure your internal procedures are sound. Some typists may balk at taking their drafts to a reader, because they don't want the word processing operator to do their final edits for them. Don't buy the machine unless you are sure your organization will use it.

12
Photocomposition

Photocomposition is an intermediate step in the printing process. The complete cycle includes design, composition, typesetting, layout, paste-up and reproduction.

The design phase involves a careful match of text, typefaces, inks, papers and function. Obviously, an annual report will receive more attention to quality than a parts catalogue.

Typically, the designer will use different typefaces and even graphics to make a point visually as well as narratively. Figure 12.1 gives a hint of the range of typefaces available. Each typeface comes in a variety of sizes, referred to as points, as well as in bold, italic and other variations. The complete typeface package is called a font.

Photocomposition is the process of converting typewritten text from 12-pitch letter gothic to the desired typeface. It involves imbedding machine instructions, or typesetting commands, into the text. This is similar to the format codes imbedded in word processing text, but much more elaborate and complex.

The process of exposing the composed text on photosensitive paper or film is the actual typesetting process itself. The output is camera-ready copy which is used to produce as many printed copies as needed.

Although it is possible to print directly from the camera-ready copy, most documents require some additional steps. The typeset copy is laid out and pasted-up to create a complete page (most machines set a column at a time). An offset plate of the page is made and used as a master for the printing process.

WHY PHOTOCOMPOSITION?

Two reasons, one aesthetic and one economic. Photocomposition does for the printed word what packaging does for a product. Thus, for marketing

Figure 12.1 Examples of Typefonts

A	A	A	**A**	A	**A**	A
No. 9 Bold Italic	Bodoni Bold	Clearface Bold Condensed	Eras Bold	Caslon Bold	No. 9 Bold	Carlton
A	**A**	A	*A*	A	A	A
Berling Italic	Helvetica Extrabold	University Roman	Le Griffe	Cut-In Bold	Neon	Stack
A	A	A	A	**A**	A	A
Souvenir Medium	Helvetica Medium Outline	Serif Gothic	American Typewriter Medium	Helvetica Bold	Windsor Outline	Cheltenham Demi

materials, advertisements, brochures and the like, it is the key to quality. It is also very useful for complex text, such as catalogues or instructions, where emphasis and arrangement can be used to enhance clarity.

Photocomposition also compacts text. Usually 30% to 40% less space is required for typeset materials. Unlike typewriter output, the typesetter offers sufficient image definition to handle this reduction. The result is a similar reduction in costs for paper, ink, handling, collating, binding, printing plates, press time, mailing and storage.

Thus, photocomposition can be cost-effective even when quality printing is not a prime factor. For example, a consulting engineering firm uses it for environmental impact statements. These documents frequently run hundreds of pages and almost as many copies. Reducing the volume of paper is sufficient justification to convert from traditional printing to photocomposition.

WHEN TO CONSIDER IT

You don't have to own a photocomposer to use one. There are many commercial printing establishments that will do your printing for you. For the small volume user, the service bureau is almost a necessity. However, there are two traditional problems with using a service bureau. First is that the printer usually rekeys your typed text to enter it on the photocomposer. This is expensive and entails an extra proofreading cycle.

The other problem has to do with control. Turnaround time, flexibility, attention to detail and quality are always more difficult to ensure when working with an outside organization. You will have coordination expenses to contend with, and you will be paying for the printer's profit as well.

For both of these reasons, many large volume users are bringing the process in-house. At a minimum, these companies keyboard their text on in-house word processors whose diskettes can be read by the print shop's photocomposer.

Other companies produce camera-ready copy in-house and use commercial printers for reproduction only. Still others bring the entire process under their own control. This entails adding equipment as well as personnel who are familiar with design, typography and printing technology.

For each organization, the point at which in-house printing becomes cost-effective is different. A good rule of thumb says do it when your annual service bureau costs equal the purchase price of the photocomposer (between one and two times the cost of a word processor).

HOW DOES IT WORK?

Before you plunge in, you should have a basic idea of how the technology works. This chapter provides an overview. If you plan to set up operations, you will, of course, need more information than this book is intended to provide. The publications list at the back has some additional sources.

The Basic Process

In photocomposition, the text is designed character by character and space by space. Characters are carefully calculated in points (vertical height) and picas (horizontal length). The point and pica measurements vary with the typeface, whether it is upper or lower case, whether or not a lower case letter has descenders, and whether or not there is associated punctuation. Justification and hyphenation decisions are also key factors in deciding the layout of specific lines.

Typesetters adjust the spacing between words (word spacing), between characters on a given line (letter spacing), and between lines (called leading). (The term leading is a throwback to the days of linotype, when bars of lead were placed between the lines of type.) Tight letter spacing, adjusting the space so that parts of one letter overhang another, is called kerning. Typesetters can do that, too.

One big difference between a word processor and a photocomposer is the control that the photocomposer gives you over the placement of individual characters.

In phototypesetting, the image of the selected character is exposed on the photosensitive paper or film. In older machines, each font of type is stored on a spinning disk, glass grid, or mylar strip. The size is controlled through a series of lenses mounted on a turret. Internal light sources expose the paper or film. Developing the exposed media is usually a clean process that does not require a dark room, special plumbing or messy chemicals.

New Technologies

Newer technologies are replacing the mechanical functions of spinning disks and rotating lenses with more electronics. An internal CRT (cathode ray tube) or other display is used to create the image of the character, which is then exposed on paper. (The process is analogous to the production of computer output microfilm.)

Storing the program required to create the character image on the CRT has been a problem. To store a single font requires as much as 20,000 characters (or bytes) of computer memory. But as computerization costs drop, this new generation technology is becoming more available.

A new development in photocomposition technology is called area composition. Most word processors and typesetters display a constant characters set on the screen. The typesetting commands change the appearance of the output, but there is no way to view their placement and relative size on the screen. Needless to say, this results in a certain amount of trial and error.

Area composition terminals recreate the actual format on the display. This allows you to see and experiment with the design and layout. Some machines even allow you to trace the outline of the space reserved for graphics on the screen, in order to fit text precisely.

Most area composition terminals must be linked to a photocomposer. This unit translates the image on the display into typesetting commands for the phototypesetter. Thus, you are adding hardware — the display terminal does not substitute for other equipment. The advantage is that you eliminate much of the trial and error during layout and paste-up. Quality control and turnaround time are improved. This technology is particularly attractive to volume users who work under tight deadlines, such as advertising agencies.

INTERFACE WITH WP

Why so much attention to photocomposition in a book about word processing? Because the tie-in is so logical. Once text is keyboarded, you have the option of using an impact printer, an image printer, or a phototypesetter for hard copy output. Each successive level gives you more flexibility of design and better quality. There is no sharp line of definition that specifies when one or the other of these technologies must be used, but typeset printing most certainly offers the best-looking product.

To interface WP and photocomposition, you have to do two things. You have to transfer the keyboarded text and format information from the word processor to the photocomposer. You also have to add the special commands for typeface, size and spacing which drive the phototypesetter.

Most word processors use ASCII code for information. This uses an eight-level configuration of on/off positions to tell the microprocessor that an A is an A, and B is B, etc. (All computers are limited to on/off representations of information.)

Many phototypesetters use a six level TTY (teletypesetting) code. Thus, the first thing the transfer may entail is code translation of the text and of the WP format commands for centering, underlining, etc. (If you are using an ASCII-based phototypesetter, this conversion is not necessary.)

Imbedding the extra typesetting commands can be done at the word processor or on the photocomposer. Using the word processor saves money, but these systems are more limited in their ability to fine tune spacing. Trial runs are sometimes required before a satisfactory print is made. Entering the commands at the photocomposer gives you better control, but typically involves more expensive equipment. You will have to do your own cost-benefit analysis to determine what works best for you. (See Figure 12.2.)

Figure 12.2 WP/Photocomposition Interface Chart

> KEYBOARD TEXT
> —on word processor
> —OR photocomposer
>
> ENTER TYPESETTING COMMANDS
> —on word processor
> —OR photocomposer
>
> LINK WORD PROCESSOR and PHOTOCOMPOSER
> —by wired electronic communications
> —by changing WP diskette to PC input on off-line "black box" device
>
> COMPOSE CAMERA-READY COPY
> —on photocomposer/typesetter

The Link

The actual transfer of text and codes from word processor to composer is accomplished in one of two ways: the medium — usually a diskette — is transferred or an electronic link is established. If the diskette is transferred, code translations are usually done on the word processor. Special software and procedures are required. The code conversion can also be done at the photocomposer or on a specially designed interfacing unit. Often called a black box, it loads a WP diskette in one side and performs the code translations. The black box is cable-connected to the photocomposer to complete the transfer. These machines are effective but expensive. (See Figure 12.3.)

If an electronic link is established, the word processor may be hard-wired by a cable to the photocomposer, or telecommunications may be used. Code translation is handled in much the same way, but the transfer is from microprocessor to microprocessor rather than from diskette to diskette.

The Hardware

There are three levels of hardware to consider. The first is a hard-wired configuration. You link a word processor to a typesetter. All text and command

Figure 12.3 WP/Photocomposer "Black Box" Interface

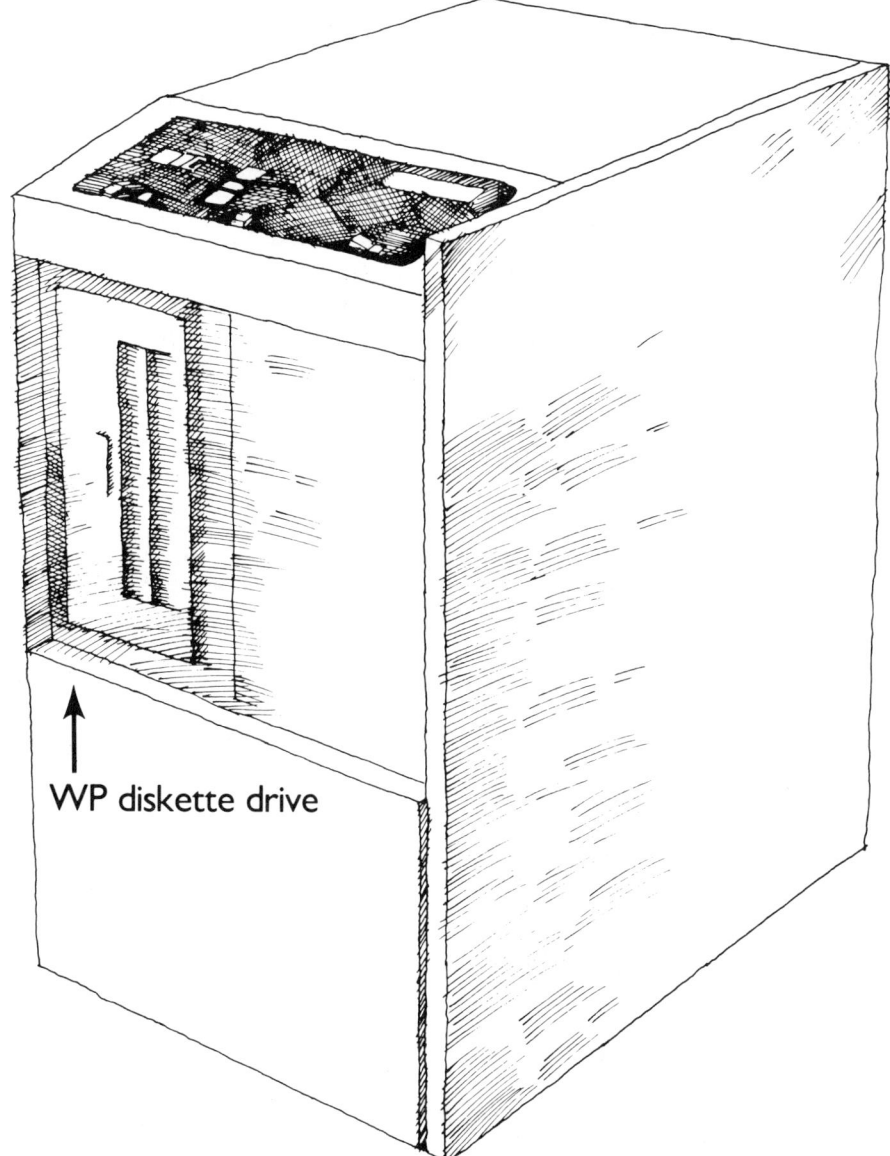

keyboarding is handled at the word processor. The typesetter in effect replaces the printer.

The next level provides a photocomposer with a screen and keyboard, but no offline storage capability. The text can be read in from the word processor or keyboarded directly on the machine (no WP interface). Some photocomposers in this category can only display and compose a line at a time. When you go to the next line, the first one is set.

Others offer expanded viewing and composing before a block of text is set. This gives you a chance to make changes. The larger the display and the buffer (internal working storage), the better.

The third level, you no doubt have guessed, adds diskette drives. It can function as a stand-alone, self-contained operation. Or it can be linked to a word processor by transferring diskettes or by telecommunications. The ability to store and revise typeset text makes this equipment very attractive to most users. (See Figure 12.4.)

Figure 12.4 Photocomposer/Typesetter

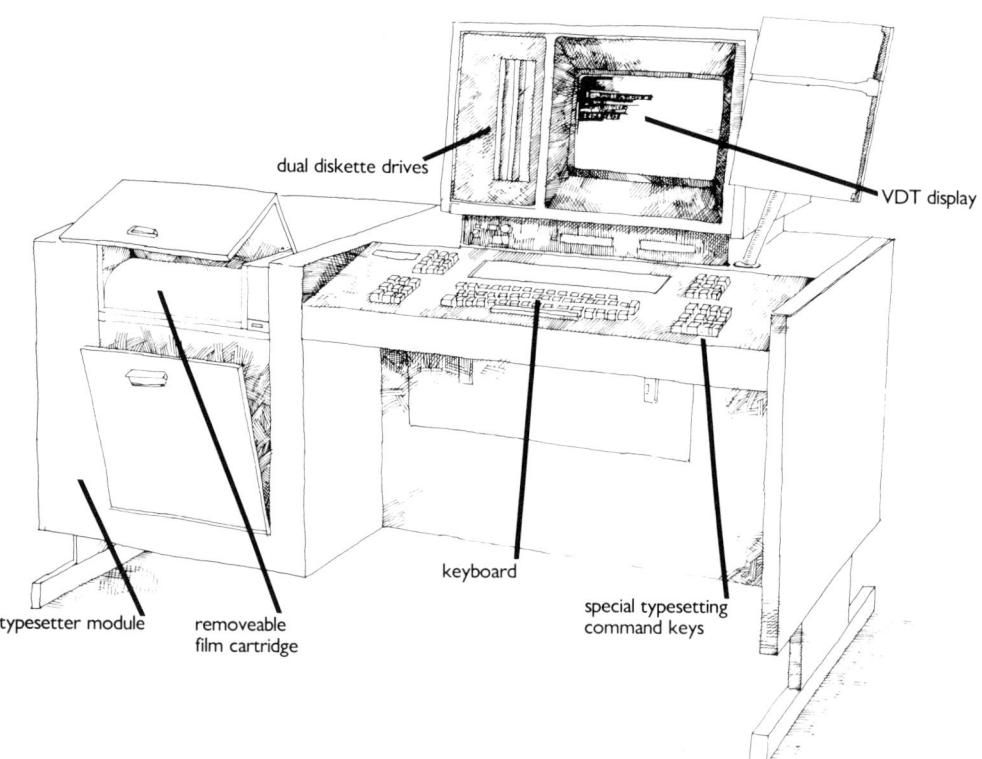

Evaluation Criteria

If you are planning to link a word processor and a photocomposer, your choice will be limited to machines which offer this kind of interface. Don't forget that special software is required to translate the word processor's text and formatting instructions for the photocomposer. The vendors must coordinate software development to link machines. If you have your heart set on a particular word processor, this will limit your choice to a compatible photocomposer.

However, you still must do an evaluation of the composition equipment. Just because a photocomposer talks to your word processor, doesn't mean it's the right machine for your application. At a minimum, check out the following.

Fonts

Number of Fonts Available: Number online at one time. Make sure you like the typefaces; not all machines offer all styles. Usually four to eight fonts are online at one time, more if you get an expensive machine. This is the number of typefaces you can set in a single operation.

Sizes of Fonts Available and Number of Sizes Online at Once: Make sure that you have enough choices to meet all your requirements.

Number of Characters per Font: Some fonts add foreign characters, such as an accented e. Special punctuation for equations can also be useful.

Special Styles and Formatting: Can italics be achieved by oblique slanting? What about underlining?

Spacing and Length

Minimum/Maximum Leading: Leading controls interline spacing. Usually expressed in points, leading varies from 1/2 point in most systems to a 1/10 point minimum, 99-1/2 point maximum, in others. A point is the smallest printing measure; there are 72 points to the inch.

Maximum Line Length: This is expressed in picas, each of which equals 12 points; thus, there are six picas to an inch. Most machines give you something less than an 8-1/2 inch print line. To make up a full page you have to paste-up columns side by side.

Width Increment: Width is expressed in ems; one em is the width of the letter M in the font being used. The width increment ranges from 1/18 em in some systems to 1/54 em in others. Small increments permit very precise control of spacing.

Word and Letter Spacing: How much control do you have in spacing? Is letter spacing manual or automatic?

Text Manipulation

Display: Displays how many lines and how many characters per line?

Reverse Leading: This is the ability to back up into previously composed text.

Buffered Storage: How much? Can you store a line as it rolls off the screen or does each line print as you go?

Tab Settings: How many tab settings? Typesetters center and format within columns, as well as flush with the tabsetting.

Auto Pagination and Auto Headers/Footers Available: Some machines add a page-depth program, automatically controlling the bottom margin.

Justification Programs: How easy is it to justify columns, inserts and so forth? Will the system insert hyphens in order to justify a line?

Hyphenation: Composers are no better at hyphenating words than are word processors. Partial dictionaries combined with hyphenation programs — called algorithms — are helpful, but you still must proofread. Algorithms on their own are not trustworthy. Complete dictionaries are good, but often slow.

Split Screen: Some very sophisticated typesetters allow you to draw from two diskettes at once, merging standard and variable material, for example.

File Management: Are there job-status indicators? How are diskette files indexed? Avoid systems with fixed-length files.

Output

Medium: Type-S or resin-coated paper or film. Positive or negative image and right or wrong reading options are available.

Process: Dry process, which uses heat, is best for office operations. Some processors are built in, others not.

Loading: Is the medium stored as single sheets? Is there a cassette? What is the capacity for a single run before the machine has to be reloaded?

Speed: Most machines list top speed in their specifications. Font and point size changes, leading and lines longer than 11 picas will slow this speed down. A demonstration is important.

Half-tones: Printed? This is usually an option only on expensive machines.

Quality: Do you like what you get?

13

Electronic Mail

In the old days, we called it telecommunications; today, we call it electronic mail. The name highlights the ability to send a message, or even a whole letter or report, without sending paper. The message may be displayed on a screen, or it may be printed out at the other end. But no paper is actually moved in the process.

DOES IT WORK WITH WORD PROCESSING?

It can. Most word processors offer telecommunications capability. However, if you are setting up message networks, communicating word processors are just one option. And they may not even be the best one. Thus, the purpose of this chapter is twofold: to explain how telecommunications works, and to give you an overview of the options available to you.

A CAUTIONARY WORD

Many users of WP buy telecommunications capability for their equipment. Some word processors even offer this as a standard feature. Very few users understand what they are getting into. As a result, they either abandon their plans for electronic mail, or they live with a system that does not truly meet their needs.

If you want to set up a fairly simple telecommunications link between a branch and central office, for example, this book probably can help you. If you plan anything more complex — data transmission, multi-point networks, or long distance communication — consult a telecommunications expert. This is a highly technical field. Don't let the fact that you can set up your own network lure you into thinking you should.

HOW DOES IT WORK?

No matter what kind of telecommunications you use, there are two basic components to the system: the link itself and the hardware. Let's look at your choices.

The Link

The link is either direct or indirect. A direct link is hard-wired; a cable goes from machine A to machine B. A word processor wired to a photocomposer or OCR reader is a good example. Usually, there is a distance limitation of 1,000 feet, more or less. Beyond that, the signal weakens enough to affect the performance of the equipment.

Any other link is indirect and goes through a telecommunications supplier. In Canada, your choices are CN/CP and TCTS. In the U.S., there is the Bell System, as well as other sources.

The telecommunications link requires a modem (modulator-demodulator) at each end. The modem translates digital information into analog signals for line transmission and then back again at the receiving end. Some modems are built in; others are separate devices.

If a machine connects directly with telecommunications this is called a Direct Access Arrangement (DAA). Others use an acoustic coupler with space to put a telephone handset inside. The modem is usually built into the coupler. Acoustic couplers are very useful for portable equipment, but are not common for permanent installations.

Newer Technologies

Most of the telecommunications described here are land-based — at least from the users' point of view. However, satellite technology is expanding, and all communications will be affected. The principal impact is likely to be vastly reduced costs, faster transmission and greater reliability.

Some vendors are already offering microwave-type communications systems for single company use. Although limited in range (five miles or less) and in reliability (bad weather poses problems), this technology is also making advances. In the future, users may be able to operate independently of the major commercial telecommunications suppliers.

Dial-up or Private Lines

As long as you are operating a traditional telecommunications link, you have two basic choices: dial-up or private lines. Each has advantages and disadvantages.

Dial-up uses conventional voice-grade telephone lines. For local area transmission there is essentially no charge. Over long distance you pay the going commercial rate. However, you may be able to send at off hours when the rates are down. In any case, you only pay for what you use. And, you can talk to anyone who has a telephone and appropriate receiving equipment.

On the minus side, dial-up lines are subject to switching. This causes line noise which may be misread as data by the receiving system. Moreover, there is a limit to the speed at which communications can be sent. For these reasons, dial-networks are usually reserved for low-volume users.

Private lines, which are leased from the commercial suppliers, are dedicated to specific users. This costs you flexibility; you are limited to the points in your network. These lines are also expensive; you pay for the line whether you use it all the time or not. However, private lines can be conditioned or "swept." All electronic interference is eliminated for virtually error-free transmission. One way small-volume users can take advantage of private lines is to use commercial packet-switching networks, which share the cost of dedicated lines among large numbers of customers.

Whether you go computer to computer, word processor to word processor, or OCR to photocomposer, your options are the same. All electronic mail systems are basically tied to the same technology.

The Hardware

For our purposes, namely office systems, we will consider that there are four major categories of communicating hardware: computers, word processors, TWX/telex networks and facsimile communications. These are the common methods of long distance transmission. Internally, photocomposers, remote workstations and even copiers may be linked together. There are also two new technologies available: local area networks and voice store and forward. Both are discussed at the end of this section.

Computers

Aside from voice communications, data communications involving computers is probably the best established form of office telecommunications. Typically, remote terminals communicate with a host computer. In distributed computer networks, the communication is more likely to be from minicomputer to minicomputer.

We will not concern ourselves with data communications here, except to raise two points. First of all, if you are transmitting data over telecommunications lines, error detection procedures are very important. Unlike text, where misreads are fairly easy to spot, they are often undetected in the case of data that is not in context.

Secondly, if you already have data communications, investigate the possibility of adding WP communications to the network. This can be accomplished by direct access or by routing WP messages through the computer. Too often, dial-up WP networks are used at commercial rates when under-utilized private lines are available.

Word Processors

There are some advantages and limitations that apply to using word processors for telecommunications. These we will discuss here. In addition, for any given machine, there are restrictions on what it will communicate with and how well. This is discussed at the end of the chapter under "Evaluation Criteria."

The most obvious limitation is that you must keyboard everything you send. (OCR offers an alternative, but only if the text you want to send can be read by your scanner.) Given the variety of materials most offices want to send, and given the flexibility of facsimile communications (described later in this chapter), this restriction is sometimes difficult to accept. Furthermore, your receiving network is limited by the need to link up with compatible WP equipment.

On the plus side, communicating WP is the best technology for providing letter quality at both ends. The equipment is also simple to use. Telecommunications adds little to the price of most word processors. Smaller companies typically do not have the resources or the expertise to establish data communications networks. WP communications provides "turn-key" technology to users who would otherwise be priced out of the market.

TWX/Telex

These are both Western Union services. They use relatively obsolete technology, and extremely slow communications speeds. Yet they are not on their way out. The reason? An enormous network of users.

TWX (Teletypewriter Exchange) is a domestic service in the U.S., Canada and Mexico. There are roughly 60,000 regular customers. Telex (Teleprinter Exchange) is international. It has over 200,000 customers in North America alone, over 1 million worldwide. All customers are listed in a directory; each customer has a unique access number. For sheer numbers of accessible addressees, these services still hold the record.

New network to come

One serious challenge to Western Union will eventually come from within AT&T. The company is in the process of creating a massive translation network. Called Advanced Communications Service (ACS), it will accept input from any WP or DP system and translate it as output to any other system. This will deal the issue of compatibility a death blow when ACS is perfected.

With ACS, your electronic mail network will include anyone with a telephone and the ability to receive digital information. No longer will you be restricted to users with similar equipment. The problem with ACS is the timetable; it is still years away. To fill this gap, private telecommunications suppliers and commercial packet-switching networks are standardizing on a single communications format, called X-25, as a means of linking up different kinds of machines. Many equipment manufacturers are beginning to offer this communications capability in order to remain competitive. If you are considering a wide-ranging telecommunications network, the X-25 standard is worth looking into.

Comparison of TWX/Telex networks

A quick review of TWX and Telex is worthwhile. (Although they are different networks, it is possible to cross between them with Western Union assistance.)

TWX is a domestic network. It is based on an 8-level ASCII code. Therefore it is compatible with computers and word processors for subsequent storage of messages. TWX transmits at 100 words per minute. Charges are 25¢ to 52.5¢ per minute, depending on distance, with whole minute billing only.

Telex is international. It is based on a five-level Baudot code, compatible with absolutely nothing. It transmits at 66.67 words per minute. Domestic billing is 22¢ to 52¢ per minute. Overseas rates are $2.00 to $4.00. Fractional minute billing in tenths is offered.

The average message length in either network is 88 words. Their slow speed and high cost make them inefficient for long documents. Although TWX is cheaper for domestic messages, the fractional-minute billing offered by Telex sometimes makes it a better deal for short transmissions.

In the not-so-old days, TWX and Telex machines punched a paper tape which was then read over the open telecommunications line. Dialing into the system was manual, repetitive and slow. Today, diskette-based systems with auto-dialing are available. A few word processors and some OCR readers are set up with direct access to these networks. If your word processor is not one of them, and if you have paper tape Western Union equipment, all is not lost. Some word processors will punch a paper tape which can be read on the TWX or Telex terminal.

Facsimile Communications

Facsimile communications, called fax for short, transmits a faithful copy of a document across telecommunications lines. Because it sends the actual image, it cannot handle digital information. Nevertheless, there are tremendous advantages to fax. You don't have to keyboard the information to send it. You can send documents you originated, as well as documents originated by anyone else. More importantly, you are not limited to text and data. You can send pictures, drawings, signature verifications, graphics, letterhead, diagrams — virtually anything you want. While the output quality will not be as good as from an impact printer, the document will be quite legible — similar to a machine copy.

Fax equipment is relatively inexpensive and easy to use. It is also easily portable. You can get convenience or high volume equipment. Within categories, you can link machines of different vendors together. This is not a given, however, and requires some guidance from the vendors. At the minimum, the two machines must transmit and receive at the same speed per page.

A fax machine links up to a telephone line. Dial-up transmission is usually acceptable. Each unit has a paper transport, which is used to load and print documents. All units send and receive, but not simultaneously. (See Figure 13.1.)

Analog Transmission

The convenience fax copiers break into two categories: those transmitting at two to three minutes per page and those at four to six minutes per page. Both

Figure 13.1 Facsimile Transceiver

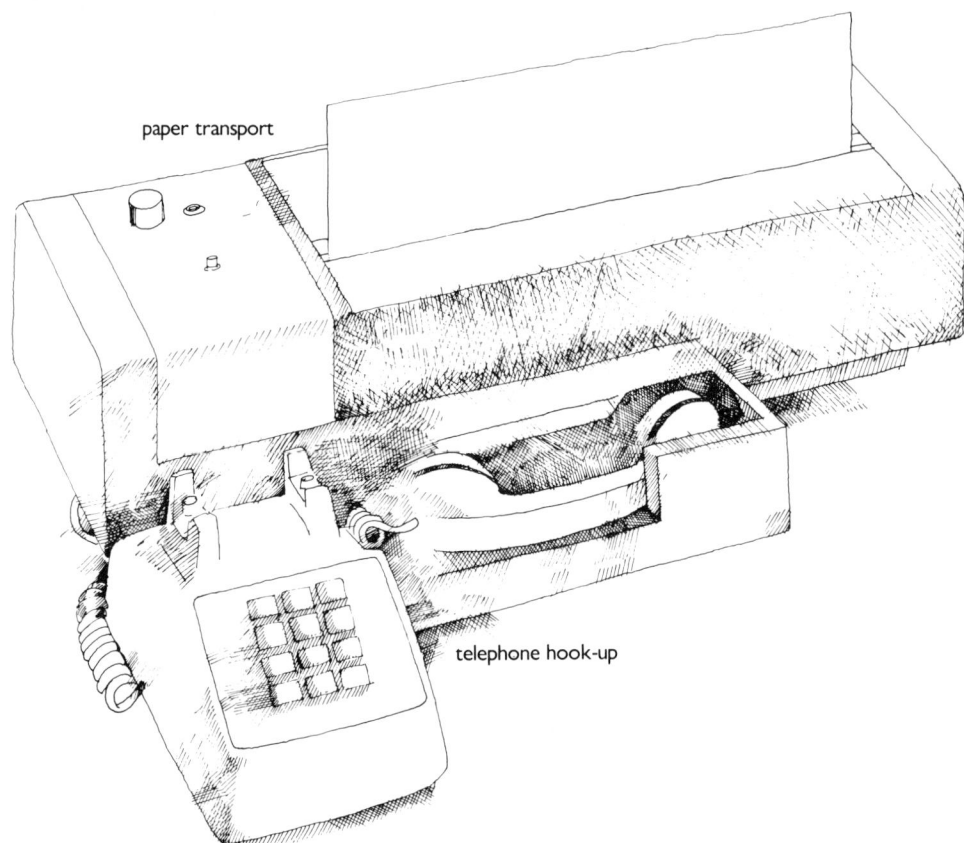

categories use analog transmission, compatible with phone lines, which eliminates the need for modems (converters). The equipment itself is relatively cheap, about the cost of an electronic typewriter. However, you do need one machine at each end. Analog fax devices scan and reproduce the *complete* page and provide reasonably good image quality.

The trade-off for cheap equipment is expensive transmission. At four minutes per page, long distance charges mount up. However, some machines have automatic document feeds and offer unattended autodialing. These can handle transmission after hours when rates are low.

Machines which transmit at four to six minutes per page are best for low volume users sending no more than 75 copies per month. These machines use FM (frequency modulation) transmission. This type of signal modulation is not susceptible to line interference.

Mid-level users, with workloads of 75 to 150 copies per month, should use machines in the two to three minute range. This is still analog equipment, but it uses AM (amplitude modulated) transmission.

Digital Transmission

High volume machines cost about four times as much as the other two categories. These systems convert copy to digital coding. As such, they require modems to tie in with telephone lines. These systems transmit at 20 to 90 seconds per page, but they only transmit what is there. Unlike convenience models, the high volume fax copiers ignore white space on the page. Thus, speed is traded for poorer image quality at the receiving end. For users sending 150+ copies per month, higher equipment costs are offset by lower long distance charges. (Some digital machines require private line transmission to ensure the quality of data.)

There are also commercial fax networks. For example, Western Union has an international service. You send your copy to them by fax or mail and they use the appropriate technology to forward the copy to an overseas recipient.

Local Area Networks

Local area networks are a product of the 80s and they are just beginning to be installed in large organizations. These are non-public signal transmission systems that can link a broad range of office equipment in a network of about five miles. LANs, as they are called for short, use an extremely broad bandwidth that permits high speed, simultaneous communications for large numbers of users.

The rationale for establishing LANs is simple: in most offices, 75% of all communications — messages, correspondence, reports — move within the organization. Not only that, 90% of all communications move one-half mile or less, and 75% move no farther than 600 feet. Eliminating paper in favor of electronic communications makes all kinds of sense. It is much more efficient to file, retrieve, duplicate and disseminate a signal than to handle hard copy. In a single organization, where compatibility can be controlled, ideal conditions for implementing LANs often exist.

LANs come in a variety of shapes and configurations. Some use coaxial cable, others work through the twisted pairs in PBX (private branch exchange) in-house telephone systems. However, they all combine the convenience of stand-alone systems (such as word processors and professional workstations) with the ability to share information files and to share high cost peripheral devices such as image printers and photocomposers.

Some LANs can carry not only digital information, but are configured to handle voice, facsimile and video as well. Ideally, this means you should be able to transmit a written employee evaluation to someone in your personnel department, annotate it with a confidential verbal message, and append a videotape of the interview session at the end. While some of this technology is in the developmental stages, and all of it is out of range for small business users at the present time, it is clear that LANs have a future and bear careful watching. If you are making long range plans for your organization, you certainly should take LANs into account.

Voice Store and Forward

This technology allows you to record a message for later distribution to as many people as you designate. It has the advantage of allowing voice communications with a number of different people simultaneously. Many of the systems are set up to compute different time zones, and to transmit a message overseas at the appropriate time. Finally, voice store and forward systems eliminate the frustration and lost time of incomplete telephone calls. If the person doesn't answer, you can leave a voice message anyway.

It remains to be seen how popular these systems will become. People have already demonstrated some resistance to telephone answering machines. Voice store and forward technology in some ways is simply an elaboration on that original theme. However, the convenience of being able to reach a large number of recipients across a broad range of time zones should prove attractive. In planning for intracompany communication, you may wish to give voice store and forward technology some consideration.

EVALUATION CRITERIA

The evaluation of electronic mail and telecommunications options is less a function of hardware than of ability to establish the right link. Often, this is software-controlled. The same hardware can be adapted to many different link requirements, as long as the right interface software is loaded on both machines.

With regard to evaluating links, the answers are black and white. Assuming you have two or more machines in your network, they either will or will not talk to each other. There are just a few gray areas, such as ease of establishing the link and speed at which the transmission takes place.

For the most part, your evaluation will net you a series of yes or no answers. The trick is to make sure you ask all the right questions. And, even if the responses are positive, ask for an actual demonstration. This is an area that definitely merits testing before commitments are made.

The list and explanatory material below should help you formulate the right set of questions and interpret the jargon of the answers:

1. RS-232 Compatible

This term refers to an Electronic Industries Association standard for signal transmission. It simply means that machine A (say a printer) can be physically linked to machine B (say a word processor). However, in order for machine A to access and process information from machine B, software compatibility is also required.

2. Communications Ports

Terminals, printers, telephone connections and other devices are linked to their word processors or computers through communications ports. Thus, if a word processor has three communications ports, it means that three devices can be linked to it.

3. Code

All digital computers, including word processors, use code to represent information. This code is composed of bits (BInary digiTs), or on/off positions in electronic memory. (A bit is the smallest unit of information recognized by a computer.) There are a number of different ways to combine bits into coded characters of information. A five-level code, such as Baudot (used in telex transmissions), uses five bits. The most common code is ASCII (American Standard Code for Information Interchange), which uses a total of eight bits per character. (Incidentally, a byte of information is the smallest amount of computer memory needed to store a single character.) In ASCII code, a byte consists of — you guessed it — eight bits.

4. Protocol

A protocol establishes the ground rules for a telecommunications transmission between a host and a receiving system. Thus, a word processor linked to a computer would have to use a protocol that the computer accepts in order to send information to it. The protocol establishes the format and timing of the transmission, so that the receiving machine understands how to process the stream of bits that come across the line. Typical protocols are 2741, 2780, 3780, TTY.

5. Convention

There are two conventions used in most WP/DP telecommunications. Asynchronous telecommunications are interactive. This means that a remote terminal can access information on a host system on a question and answer basis. In other words, you key in an information request, the machine displays a response, and you request additional information. In bisynchronous telecommunications, all the information is batched back and forth in large volumes. For example, you key in all your questions during the day; they are batched to the computer overnight. All your answers will be waiting for you when you come to work in the morning. Batch communications are typically faster, and thus more economical on long distance lines. However, the delayed response is not appropriate for all applications. Some protocols (see above) are asynchronous (2741, TTY); others are bisynchronous (3780).

6. Error-Checking or Parity

In some transmissions, extra bits are sent across the line to provide for verification of the data. They are used to check for bits that get dropped or garbled.

7. Speed

Transmission speeds are usually expressed in bits per second, sometimes written as bps or baud. A WP telecommunications transmission might go at 300 baud. Considering that there are eight bits per character, and an average of 70 characters per line, this means that there are approximately 560 bits per line (plus a few extra bits used in defining the transmission). Thus, a 300 baud transmission sends one line every two seconds or so. A 30-line page can be transmitted in about a minute, exclusive of setup time. Speeds expressed in millions of bits per second are possible in local area networks.

8. Half/Full Duplex

A half-duplex transmission means that the line can either send or receive, but not both simultaneously. In WP environments, most transmissions are at 300 baud or over and are half-duplex. Full-duplex means that the line can send and receive simultaneously. Usually, but not always, this means a transmission at less than 300 baud — unless special data lines are used.

9. Foreground/Background Operation

You do not want to dedicate your total system to a communications operation if you can help it. However, the speed of most communications is so fast that the interruption is acceptable for low volume users of foreground equipment.

10. Commercial Data Base Access

Many commercial data bases, such as WESTLAW, can be accessed using a word processor as a communicating terminal. These services offer computerized information retrieval for searching legal precedents. Their scope is beyond the reach of any single firm. Other data bases are also available. If you plan to use any of these, check that your word processor is one that your data base accepts.

Glossary

Acoustic Coupler: A data communications device that converts digital information to analog tones, and back, for transmission over telephone lines. A modem that uses a conventional telephone handset to connect with the communications line.

Algorithm: A set of software steps — or routines — that allows a word processor to calculate hyphenation decisions or character spacing for justified print-out.

Archiving: In WP and DP operations, refers to copying information stored online to offline storage media. It also refers to making copies of diskettes or disks in order to create a security copy.

ASCII (American Standard Code for Information Interchange): A code for representing characters of information — numbers, letters, punctuation — in a computer. ASCII uses a combination of 8 bits, including one for checking errors, to represent each character.

Asynchronous Communications: A telecommunications convention, or mode, for transmitting information electronically. This mode permits interactive communications between a terminal and its host computer, or any other two machines that are linked. Interactive communications are used to ask questions, such as availability of seating on an airline, and receive an answer back.

Baud: In electronic communications, refers to the speed at which information is transmitted. It usually refers to bits per second, and is sometimes written bps.

Baudot Code: A five-level code used for Telex messages. In paper tape technology, five-level code refers to punched holes on a paper tape, each row having up to five holes punched out. The various combinations of punched holes in each row allow for 26 characters and 6 format and shift commands, for space and carriage returns and numbers.

Bisynchronous Communications: A high-speed convention, or mode, for transmitting information electronically. Bisynchronous transmission is batch, meaning large volumes of information are stored up and sent all at once.

Bit: Smallest representation of information recognized by a computer. It is either an "on" or "off" position. A combination of bits is used to represent a character, such as the letter "A." ASCII code and TTS code refer to different standard patterns of bit combinations.

Boilerplate: Standard material used in many documents. Contracts, for example, carry a lot of standard language frequently referred to as boilerplate.

Boolean Logic: A method of formulating search criteria to extract information in a list or data base. It allows you to request all the records in a file which meet certain qualifications. Search criteria may be expressed in terms of greater than, equal to, or less than — as well as in combinations of greater than *and* equal to. Thus, you can ask for a list of all personnel hired July 1, 1980 *and* later.

Bubble Memory: A new information storage technology, not yet widely available. It is more compact and faster than current magnetic media storage such as diskettes. It will also continue to store information when the power is switched off, unlike main memory in most computers.

Buffer: The common term for the working memory of a word or data processing system. Information stored on media is read into the buffer, processed according to a program, and written back to the media for storage. All actual manipulations of the text and data occur in the buffer.

Byte: The smallest combination of bits needed to represent a complete character. Thus, it takes one byte to store one character of information in a computer or on storage media. Storage is typically expressed in terms of bytes rather than characters, although they are equivalent.

Canned Paragraphs: Prerecorded paragraphs which are used over and over again in varying combinations. Variable information may be inserted in blanks in the paragraphs for specific documents.

Cathode Ray Tube (CRT): A TV tube incorporated in some word processors and used to display information.

Centralization: Organizing support services, such as word or data processing, in a central location. The term implies that the service is shared among several users, and may not be directly supervised by any of them.

Character: A letter, number or punctuation mark. In computer terms, one character is stored as one byte of information.

CN/CP: Canadian National/Canadian Pacific. A Canadian telecommunications supplier.

Compatibility: The ability to interface two systems, which depends upon the availability of coordinated software. This is the essential ingredient in getting two word processors to "talk" to each other.

Compiler: The software that translates source code into object code. If a system offers a compiler, this usually means you can do your own programming.

Configuration: The hardware layout of a particular system.

Cursor: A position indicator. The cursor is displayed on the screen and can be moved at will by the WP typist. It marks the place at which keystrokes will appear when typing begins.

Daisy Wheel: An interchangeable print wheel in which the characters are arranged around the outer edge of a circle. Comes in plastic or metal.

Data Base: A comprehensive file of information stored in a computer and organized for easy analysis and quick access. For example, a data base of information about students can be used to describe incoming classes in a variety of categories, such as age, average grade point, etc.

DBMS: Data Base Management System. A software package which allows you to create and analyze a data base on a computer. The software provides the tools to formulate questions, such as "LIST all students majoring in chemistry," and to manipulate the data base to output the results.

Decentralization: Organizing support services, such as word or data processing, to support specific users. This implies that the users will not have to compete with other groups for priority attention. It does not necessarily mean that the users supervise the support systems. Supervision may still be centralized administratively.

Digital Information: Information stored on magnetic media — usually in ASCII code. In this form it can be read by a digital computer, the kind used in most word and data processing systems. For transmission over telecommunications lines, the information must be converted to an analog signal.

Disk: High-capacity, random access storage media. Disks are either fixed or removable. Most systems use some combination, in order to store disk files offline. When one removable disk fills up, another may be substituted. Disks, often called hard disks to distinguish them from floppy diskettes, are usually sealed in hard plastic containers called disk packs. Disks hold anywhere from 500 to several thousand pages.

Distributed Logic: A shared-resource system in which the microprocessors that control most text-editing and printing operations are contained in the individual workstations and printers. However, high-capacity storage media are shared.

DP: Data processing. The storage and manipulation of data. May involve management of large files of information, or may involve large-scale computations. Emphasis is on quantity of data rather than quality of format.

Drive: Used to load a floppy diskette or disk on a computer. A system which has two diskettes online will have two diskette drives.

Dumb Terminal: A workstation which has no independent capabilities. It is used solely for access to information and programs stored on a central computer in a shared-logic system.

Fiber Optics: A technology which translates digital information into light pulses which are transmitted over optical fibers. Because light operates at a very high frequency, it allows transmission of a very broad band of information. Data communications that now require bulky copper cables can be compacted into the width of a few human hairs. There are still problems interfacing digital information and light signals, but this is a very promising technology.

Field: The units of information from which a record is constructed. In a client record, fields of information might be designated for name, address, employment history, etc. A key field is one which can be used to sort the file or select specific records. For example, if name is a key field, you can sort the entire file in alpha order by name or select out all those names that start with A. Conversely, if zip code is not a key field, you cannot sort the file in zip code order. Most systems allow more fields than key fields per record.

File: A collection of records. These can be client records, accounts receivable records, etc. A file can be hard copy, or it can be stored on magnetic media.

File Management: Indexing and retrieving documents (WP) or records (DP) for processing, printing, etc.

Floppy Diskette: Storage medium for word processor or small computer, with random access storage. A floppy is protected by a special paper envelope. It can hold anywhere from 35 to 500 pages of text, depending on size, recording density, and whether one or both sides is recorded.

Foreground/Background: A foreground operation means that the screen and keyboard are dedicated to that task. Background means that while some task such as printing is being executed, a foreground operation such as editing can be taking place at the same time.

Global Functions: Global means complete or total. A global search looks for all occurrences of a particular phrase in a document. A global replace substitutes a new phrase at each occurrence. A global index is an index of all typed documents, including online and offline diskettes or disks.

Glossary Functions: Storage of commonly used phrases, such as signature blocks. Each phrase is identified by a code and can be inserted anywhere in a document by typing the code and executing the glossary command.

Hard-Copy: A hard copy file is on paper. Hard copy output means printing on paper.

Hardware: The physical components of a word or data processing system: microprocessor, display, keyboard, diskette or disk drive, printer, etc. Requires software to make it run.

Hard-Wired: Refers to one piece of equipment, such as a WP workstation, being cable-connected — or wired — to another piece, such as a central computer. (The alternative is a telecommunications link.) Hard-wired also refers to older WP equipment, in which operations were controlled by permanently-wired circuit boards rather than by a program loaded into a microprocessor.

Headers/Footers: The ability to establish constant text, such as name of addressee, date and page number, to be carried at the same place on each page of a document. At the top it is a header; at the bottom a footer.

Header Sheets: Instruction sheets which are "read" by an optical character reader (OCR). The header sheets tell the reader what typeface, line spacing and other format to look for on the documents that follow. Thus, if you want to change from scanning OCR-A to OCR-B, a new header sheet would be required. Not all scanners use header sheets; some read a paper tape, others enter new instructions at the keyboard. Still others offer one scanning option only: all instructions are contained in a single, constant program, with no ability to change.

Image Printer: Device that outputs hard copy from a word or data processing system. It uses lasers or fiber optics technology to compose the image of an entire page from digital input, and then prints it using plain paper copier technology. It differs from an intelligent copier in that it cannot be used to make prints from hard copy.

Input: Information or text entered into a word or data processing system for processing.

Intelligent Copier: An office copy machine that uses a microprocessor to control its functions. This means it can be "programmed" to do complex copying and collating jobs. Sophisticated intelligent copiers can "read" digital information from a word processor or data processing system and use this input to compose the image of a page. Multiple, collated sets can then be produced.

Interface: Refers to the linking of two machines, such as a terminal and host computer. Can also refer to the interface of two technologies, such as WP and DP.

Investment Tax Credit: A government tax incentive allows purchasers of capital equipment to write off a portion of their taxes as a reward for making the investment. When equipment is leased, the vendor has the option of retaining the tax credit or passing it on to the customer.

Justified Margins: Right *and* left margins flush, or straight (like this book), as opposed to ragged. This requires special intercharacter spacing, but improves the appearance of a document.

K: Kilo or thousand characters. Frequently used to designate storage capacity. A 256K floppy diskette holds 256,000 characters (or bytes) of information, or about 125 pages.

List Processing: Creating and manipulating a file of related information about customers, equipment inventories, personnel skills, etc. The file is divided into records, one for each customer, which in turn are divided into fields of information, such as name, address and estimated and actual sales volume. The entire list can be sorted in alphabetical or numeric order. It can also be used to prepare a list of all the customers who exceeded a certain sales volume in a given year.

Local Area Networks (LANs): Internal networks capable of transferring data, text, facsimile, video and voice communications among big numbers of users and a wide variety of office machines.

Mag Card Reader: Device which reads mag cards and transfers the information on them to floppy diskettes. So many mag card typewriters are still in use that many vendors of diskette systems offer this interface to make upgrading more attractive.

Math Processing: Sometimes referred to as math packages or arithmetic capability. Refers to functions incorporated in WP software that allow you to compute horizontal and vertical sub-totals and totals, calculate percentages and negative balances, and multiply, divide and subtract. Some math packages permit you to create and store a small program of frequently-repeated steps in a calculation.

MB: Megabyte or million characters. Used to designate storage capacity. A disk may hold 4 Mb or 4 million characters of information, about 2,000 pages.

Menus: A displayed list of the various options that a machine is ready to perform, such as Create Document, Edit Old Document, or Print. By choosing one option, a new menu may be displayed that further prompts the typist in executing all the steps necessary to create a new document correctly.

Microprocessor: A computer on a chip. A word processor will contain one or more. Technology is changing so fast that it is not possible to define the capacity of a microprocessor, other than to say it is the smallest unit that can function as a complete computer.

Minicomputer: A minicomputer is larger than a microprocessor. It typically is capable of handling multiple tasks simultaneously. However, it is very difficult to draw the line between a minicomputer and a microcomputer, as a microprocessor is sometimes called.

Modem: A device which converts digital information to analog signals for telecommunications transmission. A second modem translates the information back to digital form at the receiving end.

MSR: Marketing Support Representative. The vendor's representative for training and assistance in using WP equipment.

Object Code: The instructions for a particular program compiled into machine-readable language. This represents a translation of the source code into code the microprocessor can act on. It is not intelligible to untrained people.

OCR Reader: Device that scans printed text and translates it into digital information. Sometimes called a scanner or page reader.

OEM: Original Equipment Manufacturer. Actually the vendor who buys equipment *from* the original manufacturer and modifies it for subsequent retail sale.

Offline/Online: Refers to data storage. Offline means the storage media is not loaded on the system. It is stored separately. Online means that the information is available on the system, either in the microprocessor or on magnetic media mounted on one of the system's drives.

Output: The processed text or data from a word or data processing system.

Packet-Switching: Divides long messages into short packets of fixed maximum length. Thus, messages from several systems sharing the same telecommunications can be started before any one is finished. A short, high-priority message does not have to wait for the complete transmission of a very long message, as is the case in a traditional communications network. Packet-switching allows for shared transmission facilities and efficient use of lines.

Pagination/Repagination: Function of specifying the number of lines per page to be printed. The word processor automatically computes the individual page endings. After insertions or deletions, the page endings must be redefined. This is called repagination.

Paper-Tape Punch/Reader: Device that punches a coded representation of information on paper tape. The paper-tape reader senses punched holes in the paper in the same way that a computer senses "on/off" positions, in order to define characters. Paper-tape media is an older technology that is rapidly being replaced by magnetic media.

Peripherals: Workstations, printers, OCR devices, intelligent copiers and other input or output machines which can be linked in a shared-resource system.

Pitch: Number of characters per inch. Thus, 12-pitch means 12 characters per inch.

Professional Workstations: These high quality terminals, designed for managers and other professional staff, offer word processing, limited typesetting, graphics, extensive calculator functions and excellent information retrieval software. They perform the role of a super administrative assistant.

Program: The coded set of instructions that run a computer, be it a word or data processing system. See software.

Programming Languages: Examples are BASIC, COBOL and FORTRAN. These are English-type languages which allow you to write instructions — programs — for the computer.

Proportional Spacing: Character spacing that allows three times the space for an "M" as for an "i." This method of printing compacts text and improves its appearance.

RAM: Random Access Memory. That part of the microprocessor which is used to store the WP or DP programs in use at a given time. RAM contents can be off-loaded to a diskette and replaced with a new program. RAM is also used as working storage for text or data that is being processed for subsequent storage on magnetic media.

Random Access: The ability to go directly to information on storage media, without having to start at the beginning of a file and scan everything else before it. Diskettes and disks offer this ability; cassette tapes do not.

Recognition Logic: The software in an optical character reader that enables the scanner to translate printed text into digital information. Post-recognition logic enables the reader to edit or to reformat and modify the information to be compatible with the equipment which will use it.

Record: The complete entry of information about each entity in a file. For example, the master record for a given client, an employee's personnel folder, or a record of a sales transaction.

Redundancy: In computers, refers to a second backup system that activates automatically when the primary system fails.

ROM: Read Only Memory. That part of the microprocessor used to store the permanent operating system — the internal software which allows the computer to read and act upon the various programs loaded in RAM. PROM, Programmable Read Only Memory, allows you to change the operating system, but is found only in very sophisticated systems.

Scrolling: The ability to move text up and down or across the display, as if on a continuous sheet of paper. Allows contiguous review of more text than will fit on a single screen.

Select: The ability to select those records in a file which match certain search criteria, such as zip code or telephone prefix. Multi-level selects refer to searches such as all the records with a certain postal code and a specific telephone prefix.

Service Bureau: A firm that sells computer time to customers who do not have their own computers. Some service bureaus provide standard programs that customers can use, or customers can develop their own programs.

Shared-Logic: WP peripherals sharing the resource of a central computer.

Shared-Resource System: A WP system in which several workstations, printers and other peripherals share a central computer (shared-logic) or share disk storage (shared-storage). Some systems share both. The term shared-resource implies in all cases that the peripheral devices cannot operate independently for all functions.

Software: The programs that cause a word or data processing system to execute the user's commands. Applications software refers to programs that run specific tasks — or applications — such as accounts receivable. Systems software refers to the internal programs that enable a computer to act on the applications software. A set of programs is often referred to as a software package.

Software House: A firm that develops applications software for customers who do not have in-house programming capability. Typically, the software house does not sell any hardware.

Sort: The ability to rearrange a file in ascending or descending alphabetic or numeric order. Multi-level sorts means that a file can first be sequenced in numeric order, such as by postal code, and then in alphabetic order within each postal code group.

Source Code: The written instructions for a particular program, coded in a programming language that is intelligible to people. This is what the programmer writes down on paper and eventually enters into the microprocessor to be compiled into object code.

Stand-Alone Systems: Self-contained WP or DP systems which can handle input, processing, storage and output independently of any other device.

Status Lines: Displayed lines that tell the typist what pitch, spacing and tabs have been established for a given document, and which page and line are currently being typed.

Storage Media: Magnetic media. Magnetic cards, tapes, diskettes and disks. The information on the media is usually said to be in digital form. Paper tape is still used on some systems.

Systems Analysis: The study of an office process, such as accounts receivable, defining it in terms of inputs, procedures and outputs. The purpose is to determine if it should be automated and, if so, what kind of hardware and software will be required.

TCTS: Trans Canada Telephone System. A telecommunications supplier in Canada.

Transparency: The integration of word and data processing software into a single program.

TTS: An enhancement of Baudot code. It is a six-level code, which allows for 64 different characters and other codes. Thus, upper and lower case are possible, as well as more format codes. TTS refers to Teletypesetting Code.

TWX/Telex: Western Union telegraphic message services. TWX is domestic, Telex international.

Typefont: The complete set of letters, numbers and other characters that comprise a particular typeface, or type design.

UDKs, or User-Defined Keys: The ability to record a sequence of steps that a word processor performs, and store it under a special code established by the user. Thus, if repetitive formatting and calculations are performed each time a statistical report is updated, the commands can be stored and executed over and over at the touch of a single key.

VDT: Video Display Tube.

Vendor: The manufacturer and/or manufacturer's representative who sells the WP or DP system.

Word Wraparound: Display of an extra-long line as two lines, to accommodate the limits of the screen. Will print as one line.

Workstation: In a multi-terminal system, refers to the display/keyboard combination used by individual typists. Does not necessarily include a printer.

WP: Word Processing. The storage of keyboarded text and format information for subsequent reuse. May involve repetitive use only (power typing), or may revise text or format (text-editing). Implies high quality appearance of final output.

Publications for Further Information

Periodicals

Administrative Management. Geyer-McAllister Publications, New York, NY.

Business Week. McGraw-Hill, Inc., New York, NY.

CA Magazine. Canadian Institute of Chartered Accountants, Toronto, Canada.

Computer Decisions. Hayden Publishing Co., Rochelle Park, NJ.

Creative Computing. Creative Computing, Morristown, NJ.

Datamation. Technical Publishing Co., Greenwich, CT.

Datapro Reports on Office Systems. Datapro Research Corporation, Delran, NJ.

Desk Top Computing. Wayne Green Publishing Co., Peterborough, NH.

Geyer's Dealer's Topics. Geyer-McAllister Publications, Inc., New York, NY.

Government Data Systems. United Business Publications, New York, NY.

Infosystems. Hitchcock Publishing Co., Wheaton, IL.

IRM: Information and Records Management. DTN Corp., Hempstead, NY.

Journal of Micrographics. National Micrographics Association, Silver Spring, MD.

Personal Computing. Benwill Publishing Corp., Boston.

The Office. Office Publications, Inc., Stamford, CT.

on Computing. on Computing, Inc. Peterborough, NH.

The Seybold Report. Seybold Publications, Inc. Media, PA. (photocomposition)

The Seybold Report on Office Systems. Seybold Publications, Inc., Media, PA.

Small Business Computers. SBC Publishing Co., Montclair, NJ.

Word Processing Systems. Geyer-McAllister, Inc., New York, NY.

Books

Barden, William. *Microcomputers for Business Applications.* Howard W. Sams and Company, Inc. Indianapolis, 1979.

Costigan, Daniel M. *Micrographic Systems.* National Micrographics Association, Silver Spring, MD, 1975.

Craig, James. *Phototypesetting: A Design Manual.* Watson-Guptill Publications, New York, NY, 1978.

Illinois State Board of Education. *Word Processing Curriculum Guide.* Western Illinois University Curriculum Publications Clearinghouse, Macomb, IL.

Maedke, W.O., Mary F. Robek, and Gerald F. Brown. *Information and Records Management.* Glencoe Publishing Co., Encino, CA, 1981.

Mason, Jennie. *Introduction to Word Processing Skills and Simulations.* Bobbs-Merrill, Indianapolis, 1979.

Scott, Gregg B. *Evaluating Small Business Software.* Business Computing Press, Valencia, CA, 1976.

Seybold, John W. *Fundamentals of Modern Photocomposition.* Seybold Publications, Media, PA, 1979.

Warren, Carl, and Merl Miller. *From the Counter to the Bottom Line.* Dilithium Press, Portland, OR, 1979.

Index

Advanced Communications Service (ACS), 170
ASCII code, 159, 170, 175
AT&T, 167, 170

BASIC, 126, 127
Boolean logic, 34, 122

Canadian National/Canadian Pacific (CN/CP), 75
Case studies
  electronic typewriter, 19-21
  non-VDT systems, 22-23
  program specifications, 137-140
  special cases, 27-29
  VDT systems, 23-27
Cathode ray tube, (CRT), 14, 158
COBOL, 126
Cost
  custom programs, 129
  electronic mail interface, 168, 172
  needs analysis, 37, 46
  non-VDT word processors, 13
  OCRs, 147
  shared-resource systems, 16
  staffing, 56, 57
  VDT word processors, 67
  workstations, 131
Cost-benefit comparison, 58-62, 160
CRT. See Cathode ray tube

Data bases, 24, 133-134, 137, 177
Data processing, 3, 25, 28, 42, 63-65, 125, 128-129
  microprocessors and, 98
  word processing and, 5-6, 126-146
Dictation systems, 71-75
  equipment, 71-73
  features, 73-75
Digital Equipment Corporation, 7
Diskettes, 17, 81-82, 114
  characteristics of, 103-108
  cost of, 23
  image printers and, 112
  OCRs and, 147, 148
Disks. See Diskettes
Dura Mach 10, 3

Electric typewriters, 3, 48, 57, 147, 153
Electronic Industries Association, 175
Electronic mail, 166-177
  evaluation of, 174
  word processing and, 166, 169
Electronic typewriters, 9-12, 20, 28, 48, 98, 108, 113, 148
Equipment, 9-18
  evaluation criteria for, 93-125

Facsimile communications, 168, 171, 174
FORTRAN, 124, 126

Hardware, 103-108

International Information/Word Processing Association, 57

LANs. See Local area networks
List processing, 15-16, 22, 33-35, 50, 60, 121-123, 138
Local area networks, 100, 173

Magnetic Tape Selectric Typewriter (MTST), 4
Math processing, 15, 16, 35, 50-51
Microprocessors, 4, 160
  and word processing, 98

Non-VDT word processors, 13-14, 53, 54

OCR. See Optical character reader
Optical character reader (OCR), 101, 103, 125, 147-154, 171
  advantages of, 147-148
  disadvantages of, 148
  evaluation of, 151-154
  word processing and, 167

Personal computers, 23, 28, 101, 102, 130-131
  and word processing, 26
Photocomposition, 103, 125, 155-165
  advantages of, 155-156
  evaluation of, 162-165
  image printers and, 113
  OCRs and, 148

shared-resource systems and, 16-17
word processing and, 159-162, 167
Program specifications, 136-145

Seybold Report on Office Systems, 93
Shared-resource system, 16-17, 69, 98, 100, 104
Smith Olewine Consultants, 56
Software, 114-120
Stand-alone units, 14, 17, 69, 98, 100, 103, 104, 114, 162
Systems. *See* Word processing

Telecommunications links, 111, 125, 153, 160, 162
   evaluation of, 174-177
Trans Canada Telephone System (TCTS), 75, 167
Truax, Smith and Associates, 57
TWX and Telex, 148, 168, 169, 170
   See also Western Union, Inc.
Typing
   repetitive, 33, 39, 47, 48
   revision, 33, 39, 47, 49-50
   statistical, 47, 49, 55
   weighting factors and, 52-55

VDT. *See* Video display tube

VDT word processors, 14-15, 48, 49, 50, 53, 54, 58, 67, 110
Video display tube (VDT), 12

Western Union, Inc., 169, 170, 173
WESTLAW (U.S.), 177
Word processing
   acquisition of, 87-92
   advantages of, 6-7
   centralized, 63-67
   data processing and, 5-6
   decentralized, 67-69
   equipment, 9-18
   facilities, 79-81
   history of, 3-6
   management of, 76-79
   needs analysis and, 36-46, 57, 128
   productivity and, 7
   supplies and media, 81-83
   systems, 129-130
      analysis and design of, 132-136
      evaluation of, 83-85
   uses of, 30-35

Workstations, 97, 99, 109, 131-132

X-25 standard, 170

About the Author

Katherine Aschner is president and founder of Arcadia Associates (Seattle), an office systems consulting firm serving government and private industry in the U.S., Canada and the Middle East. A graduate of the University of Wisconsin, she was the youngest regional director of the Records Management Division, U.S. General Services Administration. Her clients now include banks, utilities, labor unions and hospitals, as well as law, mining, manufacturing, aerospace, engineering and insurance firms.

Other Titles from Knowledge Industry Publications

Electronic Mail: A Revolution in Business Communications
by Stephen Connell and Ian A. Galbraith
139 pages   hardcover $32.95
                                             softcover $22.95

Office Automation: A Glossary and Guide
edited by Nancy MacLellan Edwards
300 pages (approx.)   hardcover $59.50

Electronic Mail Executives Directory
compiled by International Resource Development Inc.
200 pages (approx.)   hardcover $120.00

Electronic Document Delivery: The Artemis Concept
by Adrian Norman
226 pages   hardcover $45.00

The Executive's Guide to TV and Radio Appearances
by Michael Bland
138 pages   hardcover $14.95

Managing the Corporate Media Center
by Eugene Marlow
215 pages   hardcover $24.95

The Future of Videotext
by Efrem Sigel, et al.
192 pages (approx.)   hardcover $32.95

Video Discs: The Technology, the Applications and the Future
by Efrem Sigel, Mark Schubin, Paul F. Merrill, et al.
183 pages   hardcover $29.95

Video in the 80s: Emerging Uses for Television in Business, Education, Medicine and Government
by Paula Dranov, Louise Moore and Adrienne Hickey
186 pages   hardcover $34.95

Available from Knowledge Industry Publications, Inc.,
701 Westchester Ave., White Plains, NY 10604